The Glue That Holds Life Together

BY WILLIAM D. BARR

THE GLUE THAT HOLDS LIFE TOGETHER
Copyright © 2021 by the family of William D. Barr

Published by TrueNorth Publishing
10380 Boundary Creek Terrace N; Maple Grove MN 55369
www.truenorthpublishingdt.com
Manufactured by Snowfall Press, Monument, CO 80132

Cover and book design: Cheryl J. Barr
Cover photo is from author's collection of photos
Retyped: Suzanne DuMont
Editing: Suzanne DuMont and Don Barr

ISBN 978-1-7376048-0-8

Scripture references are taken from the *New American Standard Bible* unless otherwise indicated *The New Testament in Modern English* (J.B. Phillips).

All rights reserved. No part of this book may be used or reproduced in any manner whatsoever without written permission from the editor.

Published in the United States of America

To my loving wife,
our five children, their lovely mates and
their children (my own grandchildren) who
have created profound relationships in my
life, I dedicate this book.

To God be the glory! May we have the wisdom
to obey His call to such relationships.

Contents

Foreword by Suzanne DuMont
About William D. Barr
Acknowledgements
Introduction
1. Let's Wake Up . . . Spiritually
2. Getting to Know Jesus
3. Profundity or Trivia?
4. The Spirit Poured Out
   These Days for a Special Reason
5. Every Natural Act Has a Spiritual Intention
6. You Are Destined to
   Give Your Body to God
7. The Most Endangered Species
8. God's Order in Families
9. Submit to Jesus . . . Not to a Teaching or Another's Control
10. Submission Protects Us From Satan
11. God's Order for Life Demonstrated in the Trinity
12. Forgiveness . . . The Key to Profound Family Relationships
13. Good News! Our Destinies Include Being Children of God
14. God Wants Us to Be Like Jesus
15. But . . . Why Don't We Love Each Other?
16. My Vision of the Church Yet to Be

Foreword

EDITORS' NOTE
JULY 2021

I was so grateful for the nudge and continued grace to retype my father's manuscript, to enable the printing of this book. As I typed, it was such a joy to listen to his voice, his enthusiasm, convictions, and concerns, as he shares the visions and words God put on his heart.

In 1986, I remember hearing of Dad's urgency to finish the book, even as his heart was failing him in those months before he finished his race. And he did it! After Dad died, Mom faithfully carried on, asking Shelly Paydon to type the final draft, which she did in 1988 or 1989. A few of us were blessed reading the manuscript over the years, but this year we felt it was time to get it in print. Though Dad wrote this in the 1980's, his message seemed timely. So Don Barr, Cheryl Barr and I teamed up to do the task. I simply typed, nudged by the Holy Spirit and Cheryl's encouragement. Don applied his Wycliffe trained eye to minor editing for clear, smooth communication that is true to the author's intent. Cheryl, a published artist and writer, was such a help managing formatting, cover design and the final printing order. As an aside, we discussed deleting obviously dated references (a 1982 issue of US News & World Report), but we decided they belonged in the book. They corroborate with Dad's views, and also give interesting historical perspective on the issues we face today.

I have wondered why we did not print this book before, especially knowing the urgency Dad felt about the message. Perhaps the delay has been ordained for the "fullness of time" when the church and the world are ready to hear about profound relationships – first with Jesus, and then with each other. The "social distancing" of COVID 19 no doubt intensified the desire among many. The need is certainly heightened by the waves of revival that are building momentum in these days. With the millions of new believers to come into the kingdom, I am convinced God is preparing hundreds of thousands of nests for their care – nests made of brothers and sisters intertwined – or "glued"– together by committed, honest, profound relating.

Dad willingly paid the price of profundity – learning the power of forgiving and going on, despite the hurts, brokenness and pain that come to the surface with such closeness. He experienced the rich rewards, saw the vital need, and earned the right to speak. I urge you to listen—to his words, his wisdom, and above all, what Jesus revealed to him. Listen with a mind and heart open to receive from the Lord, and to hear what the Spirit is saying to us today.

Jesus, our Bridegroom, is coming. Let us press on to see His heart satisfied in His Bride.

Suzanne (Suzie) DuMont

About William D. "Bill" Barr

Born in 1921 and raised in Dayton, Ohio, William D. Barr, "Bill," was greatly influenced by his father, who was passionate about making a difference in other's lives. A doctor, company VP, and church leader, Bill's father gave counsel and financial help to many throughout his life.

Bill met his wife, Wilma, "Willie," while attending the College of Wooster in Wooster, Ohio. Following graduation, they married and moved to Chicago where Bill earned a B.D. degree at McCormick Theological Seminary.

Five years later, while preaching in Wisconsin, both Bill and Willie sensed a call from God to become foreign missionaries. In 1952, with four children ages five and under, they boarded a ship for a six-week voyage to India. During their first term in India, their fifth child was born. Life in India for the Barr family was full with many happy memories. However, their third term in India was cut short due to Bill's health. They returned to Dayton where he served again in pastoral ministry.

After a few years in Dayton, they began to envision a "church without walls." Bill's heart was miraculously healed as they began to pioneer a work in the north woods of Minnesota at Okontoe Family Campsites. The program grew to included counseling through the gifts of the Holy Spirit, youth discipleship camps and mission outreach to Native Americans in Canada.

As his health declined once again, Bill began to write. His first book, *Counseling With Confidence: Spiritual Power in Counseling*, was based on seminars that he and team members taught for several years. This was published by Logos International in 1981. He wrote several other books but died in 1986 before their publication became reality. This is the third manuscript which family has published in book form in recent years.

Acknowledgements

I have many friends to thank for their help in bringing this book to publication. Especially do I thank the many counselees who have responded favorably and happily to the teachings of this book. Their new lives are an inspiration and encouragement. To my wife, whose ear I bent many a night and who graciously helped me find the right words, I am deeply indebted. My thanks to Susie Potter for typing part of the second draft and enthusiastically responding to the message of this book, and to Shelly Paydon who typed the third draft.

My special thanks go to good neighbors who loaned me their motor home, where my wife and I lived in Dallas, Texas, as I typed the first draft. Jim and Lou Schwieter are not only generous but they demonstrate profound concern for God's work.

May God bless all who desire to rid themselves of trivia in their search for God's profundity!

Bill Barr, Sr.

OTHER BOOKS BY WILLIAM D. BARR

Counseling With Confidence: Spiritual Power in Counseling
Copyright 1981 by Logos International

Life Is So Much More: Adventure Is No Illusion
Expanded edition includes family stories and memories
Compiled by Cheryl J. Barr
Copyright 2016

Baggage, Bottles and Boats
Travelogue by Bill and Willie Barr
Compiled by Cheryl J. Barr
Copyright 2020

Introduction

The crises in relationships today are epidemic. The Arabs and the Jews continue in greater intensity the feud that originated between their ancestor step-brothers. When Abraham listened to his wife's and his own doubts that God could really produce out of Sarah's barrenness a great nation of people, he set into motion the madness of the conflict we now see between Arabs and Jews. Yes...birthing Ishmael by using Sarah's handmaiden, Hagar, has created a rivalry and hatred, beginning with Isaac and Ishmael, that won't stop but breaks out as war to this day between Arabs and Jews.

But the finger pointing at the Arab-Jewish conflict also points everywhere. The conflicts between the Haves and Have-nots, White and Blacks, Northerners and Southerners in every country of the world, Protestants and Catholics, Christians and Muslims, Hindus and Muslims, atheists and believers in God, East and West, Russia and the U.S.A., and yes husbands and wives. All demonstrate a world whose relationships are in serious crisis. We who are born of the same God find ourselves controlled by hatred and fear, suspicion and mistrust, open disagreement with malice, when our lives certainly ought to be much different. Why has it been so hard for human beings to live together in God's world? Why are relationships so transitive? Why do we hate each other so much? Why don't we love each other? Yes, why don't even "Christians" love each other?

We have reached a point in history where this breakdown in profound relationships is creating not only hard-to-deal-with crises but the possibility of a world ready to blow up... literally!

In the midst of this, God clearly and urgently spoke to me about His call to profound relationships...with Him and each other. I have been studying relationships for many years and have experimented in churches, mission stations here and overseas, and most recently in a Christian community, Okontoe Fellowship, which came to life in 1971.

I am appalled at the willingness of people in all areas of life–to settle for far less in relationships than God intends us to have. I am shocked at what the Christian church, in all denominations, accepts as close-enough relationships, even when faced with our secular society and its open attacks on everything sacred. I weep when I hear leaders of evangelism teach gimmicks when introducing people to the Lord of the universe! I hear kindergarten methods of presenting the great good news of the gospel seriously taught by men whose lives should have been so profoundly touched by Jesus that they could never again settle for such childish stuff.

It is time, I believe, for the Christian church to grow up, to reach out to grasp the hand of God of this universe. It is time we put away the things of childhood and become adults in our relationships with God and with each other. It is time the Christian church once again becomes the vibrant awe-inspiring Body of Jesus Christ, who really is the Lord of all, the King of kings, before whom every knee *will* bow and every tongue *will* confess in fear and trembling when He comes in all His magnificent glory! Can't the Christian church once again become the glue that holds life together?

It is time men and women of God began singing honestly that great hymn of the church of the living Jesus:

>Rise up, oh men of God,
>Have done with lesser things
>Give heart and soul and mind and strength
>To serve the King of kings!

1
LET'S WAKE UP–SPIRITUALLY!

God has laid on my heart the job of trying to show His plan for His people as He calls us to profound relationships. The foundation of this has to be laid well, or what we have learned from God will go unheeded. That foundation is a clear demonstration of how urgent it is, no, how essential it is, to awaken spiritually! For that which God, who is Spirit, has been teaching us is spiritual truth, which, as natural persons, we cannot understand until we awaken spiritually.

This isn't as difficult as it may appear, for God, in His creation, has already created us to be spiritual, but we have lost our way as we settled for only the physical and sometimes the soulish. But we have an advantage, as God's creations, for there within us is our spirit just waiting to be called to an active life within our own busy days. How that happens exactly we must expect our Lord to reveal to us. This He does clearly through Paul.

Chapter two of 1 Corinthians contains one of those colossal revelations that staggered even Paul! He stumbled into his second chapter with words that reveal his own incredible amazement. "I did not come with superiority of speech or of wisdom." (In other words, "I really can't take credit for what I'm about to write.") I came to you (he wrote) "proclaiming to you the testimony of God...I was with you in weakness and in fear and in much trembling."

Now this picture of Paul is one we seldom recall, for Paul epitomized a strong man of great courage. Paul deliberately initiated this study of the spiritual life with evidence that it scared him stiff! It made him weak and afraid, and he found himself trembling as he realized the wonder of it all. He expanded this picture with words that betray the same new Paul, seldom known by his peers or us. "My message and my preaching were not in persuasive words of wisdom but in demonstration of the Spirit and of power that your faith should not rest on the wisdom of men, but on the power of God."

This truth God has revealed to us, too! Awakening spiritually doesn't depend upon our abilities or skills in understanding; it occurs when we actually let go of understanding and affirm Jesus as Lord and Savior of our lives, by faith, trusting Him to reveal the spiritual life He knows we need, in a dimension beyond our natural understanding.

Paul continued to describe "the hidden wisdom" of God, prepared "before the ages" for us who love Him. With sorrow, Paul wrote that the rulers of his day, had they been alive spiritually, could never have "crucified the Lord of Glory."

Then Paul quoted Isaiah, "Things which eye has not seen and ear has not heard, and which have not entered the heart (mind) of man, all that God has prepared for those who love Him." He wanted to show that the spiritual realm "all that God has prepared," is more and more being revealed, yet is far beyond the world of our senses. It is so much so that only God Himself, through the Holy Spirit, can reveal all the things He has for us. The mystery gets deeper as we step in closer to what we now know as the spiritual life. We have not received "the spirit of the world, but the Spirit who is from God, that we might know the things freely given to us by God."

Now we've reached the point where the "how" of awakening spiritually becomes clear: it means becoming able to receive the things God has prepared for us beyond our natural realm as we receive the Holy Spirit into our lives. That happens miraculously when we confess with our mouths the Lord Jesus and believe in our hearts that God raised Him from the dead. We all know that Romans 10:9 ends with the words "you shall be saved." That means the Holy Spirit moving into our lives to awaken us spiritually and making us able to start receiving the things of God! At this point Paul gave us the strongest words he could find to prove that we must step into a new dimension if we are to receive those things God has prepared for us.

Like a beacon light on a dark and foggy night, I Corinthians 2:14 warns all who would enter the spiritual life that dangerous reefs lie ahead for the person determined to hang onto his own two-dimensional living while trying to enter God's third dimension. "A natural man does not accept the things of the Spirit of God, for they are foolishness to him, and he cannot understand them, because they are spiritually appraised." Translators have used several other words to explain this spiritual truth—"appraised" can also be rendered "examined" or "discerned"; the latter seems to best separate spiritual reality from natural understanding. A new dimension–of receiving from God things the natural mind cannot receive–opens up to believers.

By our confessing Jesus and believing God, the Holy Spirit opens up a wide limitless world just beyond man's comprehension. Suddenly all things of God that seemed foolish now appear wonderfully real! Through our new spiritual discernment, that which we could not understand, now excites our whole being in ways we formerly could not have handled. Waves of awe and joy burst upon us as we discover that all God has for us is wonderful beyond imagination.

"Things of the Spirit of God" (2:14) include the gifts of the Spirit listed in 1 Corinthians 12, including God's words of wisdom; God's words of knowledge; God's faith to understand (comprehend and discern) all things; the gift of God to see people physically and spiritually healed; eyes (spiritual and even physical) to witness God's miracles, and then the power to actually perform those miracles; these connect us to

God in unique and wonderful ways. Then, as prophecies become a brilliant new channel God uses to teach us, comes the exciting awareness that God still speaks to His loved ones.

While all these gifts are rising in our lives, God wisely grants us discernment of spirits so we will not be led into satan's*[1] lies, and so we will instantly recognize the Holy Spirit as He begins making us over into the image of Jesus! One of God's surprising gifts is the ability to speak in tongues we do not understand, and yet, as they are spoken by the power of the Holy Spirit out of our own mouths, glory begins to awaken within us. And God, understanding how all of this is so new to us, often will give us an interpretation of tongues so we will know we are actually speaking the truth of God.

I remain amazed at how God expands our minds and explores our spirits in ways that allow us to touch Him and finally awaken to the wonder of His plan for us and the completeness of it all. We now find ourselves open to God's whole truth in His Word and as He speaks today through the gifts. The totality of His Word, the unity of it, the fullness of the truth in it just breaks in on the person who awakens spiritually. Then a new, intimate relation starts growing between the Almighty God of the Universe and our own little selves!

Can you see now why it is urgent that you join me in awakening spiritually as we study God's call to profound relationships? The thoughts that follow through this book are not coined from the wisdom of my life or the world in which I live. They are revealed truth from the God of us all, and if you would enter into the great adventure of receiving His truth, do come and join me in that awesome third dimension of the Spirit!

1

I have decided that I will never dignify the name of evil by capitalizing the name of the enemy of God. Hence, whenever his name is used in this book, he will never be honored with a capital letter heading his name!

If we live only with what comes naturally, we can shut ourselves off from God's plan for our lives. Ephesians 4:17 (Phillips) says, "Do not live any longer…blindfold in a world of illusion…cut off from the life of God." When we try to live by what our best thinkers tell us is right, we often come up short-changed. We are destined to be children of God, not just people trying to make the most out of life by our own efforts. The thoughts of our world's best thinkers and leaders often turn out to be less than profound and more often controlled ideas that crowd us into new bondages. When we get discouraged trying to do what some person tells us is right, we often end up bending the idea to fit our own selfish desires. This leaves us to face life with bent ideas which more often than not lead us into perversions of truth.

The Christian life is a life lived in the Spirit, connected to God so completely that we begin to understand, no, to *discern* spiritually, what God has in His plans for us. Until this happens, friend, what God has been revealing to me in this book will appear foolish to you. I am absolutely convinced that the Baptism of the Holy Spirit took all my intellectual searches and opened a new door of truth that was not the product of my mind or other persons' minds, but rather truth out of the heart of God!

I invite you to join me in an adventure of awakening spiritually and becoming able to receive the "things of the Spirit of God."

2

GETTING TO KNOW JESUS

Who can separate us from the love of Christ? Can troubles, pain, or persecution? Can lack of clothes and food, danger to life and limb, the threat of force of arms? ... I have become absolutely convinced that neither death nor life, neither messenger of Heaven nor monarch of earth, neither what happens today nor what may happen tomorrow, neither power from on high nor a power from below, nor anything else in God's whole world has any power to separate us from the love of God in Christ Jesus our Lord!

Romans 8:35, 38, 39 (Phillips)

So many people come to us with grave doubts in their lives, wondering if Jesus really loves them. Their relationship with Jesus is not profound at all! Often these are people who have been leaders of the church, people who have been active in the charismatic movement, yes, people who have received the Baptism of the Holy Spirit. We hear them believing the lies of satan as they question Jesus' love for them. I want them all to have burned in their memories the message Paul wrote so powerfully in his letter to the Romans: "Who can separate us from His love?" Can disappointments? Can rejection of the people you think love you? Do you feel rejected and sat on to the point where you think you cannot be loved by even Jesus–that there's something so wrong with you God can't possibly help?

These are the cries of people's hearts as they come: "Why am I so bad?" "Why doesn't Jesus help me?" "Why am I not loved and understood?"

And we say over and over again, "You're listening to the father of lies, not to Jesus, the Savior, the lover of mankind!"

God has been teaching us a great deal about relationships with Him and with each other. I had the honor of going to the point of death in September of 1980. I had the honor, I say, of seeing satan routed and Jesus move in! I want to tell you a bit about that time for in that encounter, something happened to my understanding of who Jesus is.

We've all gotten the idea that Jesus is one who if we measure up, might love us. We've somehow gotten the idea that if our marriage appears all right, then God will bless it. We've thought that if we can keep our children's noses clean and out of mischief most of the time, that will just make them become great men and women of God. We've imagined that if we just measure up to some of Jesus' expectations, He might possibly consider helping us in times of great need.

That's not at all a picture of the Jesus I know. Jesus says He doesn't measure us anymore. He doesn't judge us. He only loves us! I want to try to show this in a way that has finally reached deep into my soul and shaken me to the roots of my being.

One of the struggles we have in our lives is that we have highs, in moments of great worship, for example, but the next day we are hit with a great low–perhaps some bill can't be paid or the car won't start, or we have a spat with our wife or husband, and the high is gone. Then we wonder why we so quickly lose the glory of God. I'll tell you why; we don't really know Jesus! We picture Him as something austere. Something we can try to reach up to, but not really understand. We see Him as someone who can look at us but not really understand our sorrows. We look at Him and say, "Oh, He never had to pay a bill." When others talk about Him being a Man acquainted with sorrow, we question in our hearts whether He really did experience sorrow. After all, He knew He was going to come out of the grave. Yet the Jesus too few of us know reaches into our lives to help us. The real Jesus desires to go through all of life with us. Nothing can actually separate us from the love of Jesus.

    I learned this truth in a strange, deep way. After my third heart attack, the doctors and surgeons saved my heart from exploding by doing a triple by-pass. They stripped a large vein from my left leg; the scar still reminds me that it helped save this old heart of mine. A lot of strange things happened during those days of recovery, and I developed a deep staph infection which couldn't be located. I started losing weight and I rejoiced, not knowing how much I would lose before it was all over. I went down to 135 pounds, a new experience for this always-a-bit-overweight person. I couldn't eat for three weeks and often thought, "At last I've discovered how to get weight off quickly!" But the doctors were deeply concerned as they sought to find the source of the infection.

    I was beginning to have terrible nightmares. I would wake up and pray, "Jesus, don't let this go on in my life." I wasn't sleeping much, as you can imagine. Every movement created excruciating pain. Going through those times brought me to one day–yes, in broad daylight–when suddenly I saw two demons hanging over the curtain next to my bed. I had always heard that demons are little green creatures about ten inches tall. That's what any people I know have seen, but I saw what looked like grey pancakes, with great black eyes, hanging over that curtain, staring greedily at me. I looked at them and knew exactly who they were: death and infirmity, and I knew exactly what to do, so I said to them, "You can both leave, because Jesus has promised to restore me. So just get lost, in the name of Jesus!" And they left immediately!

    After that strange experience, I called my family together and asked, "Will you do spiritual warfare for me? I want to have something beautiful at night instead of all this messing around fighting nightmares!" So my family came and stood around my hospital bed. My son-in-law, Rob, and my son, Bill, came and stood by my side, and two of my daughters, Suzie and Nancy, joined by my darling wife. As they held hands about my bed, they did spiritual warfare, pleading the blood of Jesus over me, and drove away the forces of evil when I was at the point of dying. God was faithful! I never had another nightmare–they left, and in their place, Jesus moved in. The Lord Jesus moves in remarkable ways to touch people. I pray you will expect this in your lives.

He came and talked to me one night, as I sat there in bed with a great deal of pain. I said to the Lord, "What are you trying to teach me?"

He said very quietly, "Suffering."

I thought about His words for a while and then asked, "Well, how much can a man stand in the way of suffering?"

I was really racked with pain, and He very gently replied, "If I were to ask you to suffer unto death, could you die with dignity?"

As I worked that through my pain-filled mind, I had to admit to Jesus, "I'd probably blow it, and you'd have to come and help me."

It was then that He spoke these strange words just before launching me into a new dimension of conversation: "You don't understand a word you are saying."

I thought I knew Jesus intimately. But as He took me into another dimension of communication, the wonder of who He really is began to explode on me. He began to reveal to me who He is. Complete thoughts poured in on me in waves of wonderful awareness. "Don't you realize," His thoughts were filling me, "that you would die with dignity because I would die with you? Don't you know that I would never leave you? Don't you understand that I'm suffering with you right now?" The wonder of who Jesus is began penetrating into my deepest being as He continued to feed me with thoughts beyond my comprehension. To realize how intimately He loves us, to see what He does for us all the time, comforted me in ways I can't yet fully express!

I was aware of Him saying that He hadn't yet asked me to suffer unto the shedding of blood. (This was two days before I began to bleed internally.) I remember my thoughts as I tried to understand what it meant to suffer unto the shedding of blood.

"No, Lord," I responded, "I haven't been sacrificed yet. I haven't had my head cut off yet. I haven't been persecuted for righteousness' sake as I fully expect to be in the years ahead. I know that, Lord."

While I was exchanging these thoughts with Jesus, all of a sudden He was in my presence on the cross. He was so close I could have touched Him. As He was leaning out from the cross just over my bed, I saw that his shoulders were out of joint. His head was bleeding. The crown of thorns was jammed down hard on His head. His back was in ribbons. We sometimes forget that Jesus was whipped with the cat-of-nine tails, but at that moment there was no forgetting! I saw Him almost black, for most of His blood had gone from Him. He was looking right at me, head bowed, torn to pieces. The spear thrust that we read about...a thrust, no, a vicious gash. I saw it. His insides were spilled out on the ground.

While I was trying to recover from the terrible experience of seeing my Lord suffer that way, trying to grasp the meaning of it all, He moved me in the Spirit to another scene. I found myself in a tall tower at night. I was hanging upside down in that tower and Jesus was hanging there with me, also upside down! His hair was tied in a knot hanging below Him. He was smiling! His hands were bound, like mine, and we were wrapped up like mummies as we hung there. My left shoulder was right against Him; I can feel it yet today. The living Jesus, who had just gone through death on the cross, smiled at me and said, "You know, they did everything they could to destroy me, but that is impossible!" And then His shoulder rubbed against mine.

Then the new dimension began, as an awareness in my heart took form, and I realized I didn't really know Jesus as well as I thought I did. Since then, I've lived my life with Jesus. I've spent the last years of my life in the deep walk of the Spirit.

I live in the memory of the suffering Christ, with His shoulder against mine.

Do you understand Jesus a little better? Do you see why I say to you, you can't live in these days and the days that are coming up, soon to be filled with troubles and trials, with a Jesus you may barely know? Remember this well, loved ones! Expect Jesus to go through your sufferings with you. Anticipate Jesus stepping into your room and speaking to you. Let Him do this for you. Don't continue to just play the game of going to church. It just will not work for what lies ahead. Such games will not stand up under the test of trials and tribulations that are coming upon us all. You will not stand up under that unless you know Jesus intimately. Unless we all have a profound relationship with the living Jesus, there is no future for us who are Christians.

Vision of Sadhu Sundar Singh, India
I thanked the God…my Master, for rescuing me…
I opened my mind and spread it out before Him!
Joy of the companionship of my Master came to me!!
Pleasure filled me and happiness…
I finished my prayer and opened my eyes.
I saw a Person standing before me; tall and fair,
With perfect face, keen-eyed and from head to foot
He was bright…bright!

Out of Him…lightning flashes of live truth struck into me!
Love full-strength burst from Him!
Love full-strength rushed into me!!
I fell at His feet…His Spirit and His Image entered me!
He filled me with light…with love…
Then He was gone…
Now He shows Himself to me in all places, in all things!
My eyes see only Him!
I listen to His voice…that wakes love…
It is He, in the beating of my heart…in my breath…
In the sun's rays…in the dew.in the wind's moving…
In the bird's rising…in the insect's chirp…
In the river's chant…in the green breadth of the fields
And the height of the trees!
He only…He himself…
Who was and is now and will be endlessly!!!

3

PROFUNDITY OR TRIVIA?

After my long nights of struggling with nightmares and finally getting free, each night I waited with deep anticipation for Jesus' visits. These were good nights with Jesus sitting on my bed in that hospital room. Everybody was asleep except for the quietly moving nurses. An occasional bit of conversation crept into my drugged mind as several nurses exchanged bits of gossip or even quiet reactions to very sick patients.

Lying there drifting in and out of sleep struggling how to lie without pain, to move without stirring up the pain that tore me apart, wondering what was really happening to me–those were the moments when Jesus often surprised me with His brilliant presence. Many people have asked me what Jesus looked like as He appeared before me. He came in different ways at different times, but the most common picture I have of Him is identical to that experienced by so many who have died, gone to heaven, and returned. Marvin Ford, in his book, *On the Other Side,* described what I have seen. At first I did not see Jesus as He came to me. I just got that awesome feeling of His presence, the warm glow of knowing He was coming into my room, a strangely free-from-fear contentment of knowing all was well. Then, as I found myself waking to the reality that He was there, the visual awareness of something intensely bright, impossible to look upon with human eyes, would begin to shine on me. All I could see with my eyes was a brightness, pure and intense. Yet there was no sense of pain or fear of having my eyes hurt from the intensity of the brightness. There was a totally wonderful warmth and beauty to that light. The word "presence" best expresses what I have experienced with Jesus and there is never a question as to whose presence. Many people have described this presence as sort of oblong in shape, like an over-sized halo surrounding the whole body of Jesus. I have been able to identify with such descriptions, but most of all with those who experience the full awareness that Jesus is clearly standing before them. There is no mistaking that presence. The gentleness, the warmth of love that reaches out to one there in His presence, is beyond full description. The straightforward way Jesus spoke, yet so clearly in love, was always startling to me.

Out of that glowing presence I heard, "I'm going to teach you about profundity tonight. I'm going to teach you profundity, and I want you to see the difference between profundity and trivia." I lay there wondering what the true meaning of profundity was. Then He took me through a most interesting night, relating to me a parable, and I was in that parable. It's really fascinating to see how the Lord loves to teach, and the intimate way He teaches. Now I had known Jesus pretty well by that time, having gone through a number of shaking experiences with Him. So I expected all kinds of good and exciting things. I wasn't disappointed at all in the way He worked with me.

He said, "You are going with me on a trip right now."

I thought, "Here we go…I'm going to get up to heaven and come back and tell my friends all about it!" That's what I really thought Jesus was about to do. I knew He wasn't taking me through death, for just a few nights prior to this eventful night I had openly asked Him to take me on into heaven. I was suffering so much and hanging between life and death, and when He was standing there with me, I came right out and asked, "Jesus, why don't you take me on in now?"

His immediate response was, "Don't ever say that again! I promised to restore you, and I shall restore you!" I recall how rested I felt then and yet how disappointed I felt, too, knowing what joy and freedom from pain it would be to go on into the glories of heaven! I remember how blessed I was to know that satan had been routed, and Jesus had now reassured me of His plan to restore me. I knew right then that I was not going to die, even though all the doctors and nurses and my own family felt I was about to do just that.

    Then Jesus was again saying, "I want to take you on a trip. You're the president of a corporation on the edge of Canada. Everybody has everything in common. You have sisters and brothers and children and grandchildren and many others working there with you. You happen to have one sister who is married to a French-Canadian, and she lives in Canada. You are going to visit her and you're taking all the family along. A strange thing about your sister is that you have always made her speak French in your presence when she comes to visit you." I couldn't figure out the point of that statement. He continued to describe the situation we were in. One of the girls walked by wearing a beautiful dress, looking really pretty, and someone said, "My, don't you look beautiful!"

    She replied, "Yes! And I thank you for it. You've been so kind to provide everything for us." She had a gentle, sweet spirit.

    The parable goes on with us going to Canada in a couple of motor homes, and as we got settled there in a campground, along came our sister who spoke French. Now none of us spoke French, but we made her speak it. I couldn't understand where we were heading with all these sets of circumstances and strange relationships, but the Lord knew and took me deeper into the parable. As we were sitting there, a bunch of the grandchildren were running around with some friends. A little boy walked up and said, "What's the matter with Aunt Nancy that she's speaking that dumb, silly language none of us can understand?"

    Right then Jesus put me in that situation and said to me, "Now, teach him!"

I said, "Come here! What makes you think you're so unusual that you can talk about Nancy that way?"

"Oh," he cleverly said, "I can throw a jackknife pretty far."

I then asked, "Well, what makes you so different from little Johnny over there?"

"Oh," he said, "Johnny has proved he's really smart!"

All of a sudden Jesus spoke forcefully, "Trivia! All of these relations are trivia."

I turned in surprise and said to Jesus, "I don't understand."

Then He spoke to me, "Tell this child, 'You are who you are because you belong to God. Nancy is who she is because she belongs to God.'" And then directly to me He said, "You are who you are because you are mine!"

As He spoke these words I was caught up in a feeling that these were deeply significant words for my life and for all who finally discover that Jesus is the Savior but also profoundly the Lord of life. He kept on with words that ring in my memories and caused me, for the first time, to understand something of His deep concern for the way we all live. He said, "I'm tired of the trivial relationships people have. I'm tired of the barriers you've set up. I'm tired of the things you have created to separate yourselves from each other. I'm tired of what your trivial ways tell you you're good for. You're only good because I make you good. You are right only because I make you right. You are mine!

"I'm calling you to a more complete understanding of relationships with every person. It isn't because you care about them enough to see that they get enough to live on, but it has an intrinsic value because they are mine. The relationships that are trivial are like the scum that we scrub off our bodies every day, because it is not of God. That which is of God penetrates." Then Jesus concluded with these profound words: "Knowing me is all there is!"

Can you see why I ask you if you really know this Jesus who spoke such words? Do you know Him intimately? That's all there is! If you don't have that intimate relationship with Jesus, you don't have *anything*!

A strange experience in the hospital made it possible to recall exactly everything I have reported about profundity and trivia. A beloved, long-time friend of mine, Dr. Bill Smith, a veterinarian who often calls himself the "Hog and Dog Doctor," often came to my bedside. One morning I awoke to see Bill standing by my bed asking a strange question: "What has He been teaching you? He told me this morning to bring my tape recorder." Now, I could barely speak in those days, as my voice was hoarse and very difficult to hear, yet, as Bill put that little tape recorder next to my mouth, out would come all the teachings Jesus was giving me in the quiet of the night. In my drugged and extremely weakened condition, it was amazing to discover how complete the messages were when we transcribed them months later. I often wondered, and even questioned the people who were recording the messages, if I was hallucinating or not making sense. But the recordings proved clearly that Jesus really had been teaching me wonderful new truths that need to be proclaimed to a very sick world.

As I heard those recordings and began to study the transcriptions with my wife, I started searching out a deeper definition of profundity and trivia. I got out a good dictionary and began opening my mind to what those words really can mean. Webster says *Profound* is the root of *profundity*, and it means "marked by intellectual depth, as a profound discussion of good and evil; deep or intensely felt, as profound grief." Profound also means "thorough going," as "profound changes in our mode of living." The definitions were beginning to penetrate my mind, making me realize the many facets of what Jesus had spoken. Each further definition showed me that Jesus clearly knew I would look up *profundity* in the dictionary and would then get a much broader understanding of what He was teaching.

Then I looked up *trivia* and whole new depths of what Jesus was calling us away from began to awaken in my mind. Webster says, *trivia* is "unimportant matters, trivialities, trifles." That word *trifle* began to stir in me questions about what Jesus really meant when He used the word *trivia*. I thought of *truffles* and played around with that until I remembered they are some kind of European delicacy. So I turned again to the dictionary and looked up *trifle*, and the definition shocked me when I considered relationships and what they ought to be. *Trifle* means "to dally, to play fast and loose, as with a person's affections." *Trifle* means to treat without earnestness, without full attention or definite purpose. I was shocked!

Think of relationships between people you know, including your wife, or husband, or children, or associates, or the people who sit with you in church, yes, those who live in your neighborhood. Do you have to measure them the way I had to, as trifling relationships? "Trivia," Jesus said.

4

THE SPIRIT POURED OUT THESE DAYS FOR A SPECIAL REASON

As I think of God's call for us to have profound relationships with each other and especially with Jesus, I know why the Holy Spirit has fallen on us in these last days. I know why Jesus baptizes us with His Spirit, and why the gifts of the Spirit are functioning. God intends us to be closer to Jesus because of the gifts and by the movement of the Spirit within our lives. It's not an alternative lifestyle. It's absolutely necessary for the growth God expects of us.

All my life I have been working in the church, both in America and in India. The large majority of the people I have grown up with in my church would consider me strange since Jesus and the power of His Spirit began to govern my life. I love the church and the people in it and, yes, even some of its traditions. I've been a part of the church all my life and I still cherish it, for it brought me to Jesus! Now that Jesus has taken me and many wonderful friends and family members into a fresh new kind of life in the Spirit, I want that new life for every person in my church today!

This life is ours to have even as the first-century church grasped it and turned the world upside down. There has always been a baptism of the Spirit available for every believer. It's not just some second hope or another way of acting out our faith. The life in the Spirit which God entreats us to enter as He calls us to profound relationships, happens to be the *normal* Christian life! It belongs in the center of our traditions as denominations. When I consider how few of my loved ones are open to this gracious act of God, I know that we have failed them. Our witness of what God is about has been too trivial. Too many of our people have thought of us charismatics as only demonstrative hand-holders, hand-raisers, embarrassing huggers, and dancers in the aisles of the church! Our relationship with Jesus and with each other has not been communicated.

    I am tempted to be crushed by our churches' failure to understand what we know to be the heart of Christianity. But I think it is time we brush aside those feelings and help the churches to awaken to this new life in Jesus! Many people these days, in reaction to the traditional churches' rejection of their new life in Christ, want to write off the church and its blindness to the truth. I hear many poking fun at the way our churches so readily accept humanistic liberalism and shut their eyes and ears to the real call of God. I can't join them, for I still stand in awe of the church, even in its blindness, for the church is truly the Body of Christ. Yes, the Body of Jesus Christ, with perhaps the huge majority of the members not knowing who Jesus really is. That breaks my heart, for it's like belonging to a body and not being a part of it. It's like not being aware that when the heart is failing, the rest of the body - arms, legs and torso - are in danger of dying. It's like wondering why a foot in the body of Christ grows numb when the foot is suffering from lack of circulation because the heart has not received attention. The Body of Jesus Christ is suffering deeply because the members have become oblivious to their urgent need of each other. The leg thinks the arm doesn't look like a leg and therefore doesn't belong in the body. The arm forgets that the legs make it possible for the arm to move about doing the things it believes important. The church is suffering today because its members, in their obsession with how they want to live, have forgotten they are members of a vital Body that is, in truth, Jesus Christ.

    The movement of the Spirit is calling us today to be real

with people, be profound in our conversations, be deep in our relationships, and cast out forever the trivial relations we too often accept as the way things are these days.

There are churches awakening to being the Body of Christ in very practical ways. In one church I know well, a new group of young adults, all baptized in the Spirit, have been meeting regularly and studying what it means to be the real Body of Christ. They have been open to the gifts of the Spirit, and God has blessed them with grand times of worship and study. But recently one of the couples has been struggling with marital problems. Much prayer and counsel have gone into the lives of that couple, but as the anger of one surfaced and strange unchristian attitudes and actions became violently evident, the group hesitated to interfere, questioning how much they really should do. When the anger forced one member to leave home for a night, it seemed the world had stolen another Christian away from the truth. But in the midst of that I was able to suggest that the group start actually being the Body of Christ by reaching out to both the husband and wife in love and understanding. I suggested that the men in the group go and stand with the man in his anger and just love him, not bawl him out or criticize him, just be there feeling his frustration and anger.

At first the group felt that was too much pressure to put on the man, but finally decided to do it. Three of the men went to visit the husband as his anger was again tearing the family apart. Another couple in that group started meeting with the troubled couple and encouraged them to let Jesus into their troubles. As the battle raged between husband and wife, instead of being left *alone* to hurt each other more and more, the Body of Jesus, being that small group, began sharing the hurt and anger and frustrations as members of one another. *This is what the Church is meant to be.* This action, this loving concern, is what God is calling us to. This is life in the Spirit. This is why the Spirit has been poured out on all flesh in our time.

Another reason the Spirit has been poured out is that we really are approaching the end of time. Times of tribulation are coming upon us whether we believe in them or not. It doesn't matter when we expect the rapture of the church to occur - we are all going to face trouble. World crises are upon us already and more political and economic trouble is ahead as the world dashes after humanism. The wars won't stop! Aggression increases everywhere we look. The blatant blasphemies of our immoral society demand control of all of life. Confusion dominates TV and radio, commentators drawing from a great reservoir of ignorance. These troubles face us and cause tribulation in our hearts and lives.

For such times we have no hope of survival, if we don't have a deep relationship with Jesus. We Christians would fail like the rest of the world. We'd cry out in agony and despair, "Why does God do this to me?" But He will provide for us everything we really need! Remember what Jesus said to me in the hospital: "You are who you are, because you are mine." When we belong to Jesus Christ, no power in heaven, on earth, or below the earth can separate us from His love! But we must become part of His plan for us or we are lost.

How can we understand it all! What does His Word say? "God...purposes in his sovereign will that all human history shall be consummated in Christ, that everything that exists in heaven or earth shall find its perfection and fulfillment in Him. And here is the staggering thing–that in all which will one day belong to Him we have been promised a share." (Eph. 1:9-10 Phillips).

Do you want that share of God's glory planned for believers? Or are you just crossing your fingers, hoping to get into heaven somehow? We used to chuckle about the church member who said, "I go to church to make sure I get to heaven, just in case life after death is true, because I don't want to be shoveling coal in the hereafter." I chuckle no more. For now I know: without a personal relationship with Jesus, without knowing Him intimately, there is no heaven for anyone. I'm stating a terrible fact. Yet it is the most wonderful truth I can say to anyone. You can't face the present and future of this out-of-step-with-God world, let alone face life beyond, with just a casual understanding of who Jesus is. You can't just know where He came from, who He was and how He fits in with all the other greats of the world. You've got to know Him, the only Savior, the one who goes through even death with you, the one who suffers with you, yes, the one who says to you as He said to me: "You know they did everything they could to destroy me, but that's impossible!"

For such times as are ahead, we must each know Jesus intimately. I honestly believe the culmination of history is close upon us. You can argue about the length of time until Christ returns, but I don't argue anymore. God, in His gracious mercy, has allowed us to read all about it in His mighty Word. Suddenly a lot of us are getting a picture we never took the time to see before. We are beginning to understand more of His plan for the climax of history. I used to think that study of the end times belonged to the old white-haired scholars of our church. I remember the struggle I had as a young missionary in India. I used to say to an old missionary, "Oh, you take care of that hard-to-understand time yet to be, brother, that's fine. I'll get on with building the Kingdom of God now." How little I knew!

Now, thirty years later, I believe we are so close to the end of time that Jesus is saying loud and clear, "Get rid of trivia. Get it out of your lives! Have no part of it at all. Get now into profound relationships, for without such there is no survival ahead!" To survive in the days ahead of us, with money values changing, with governments rising and falling, with all the things happening around the world, we will need to give and receive from each other. We will need to care for each other. We will need to love each other, to deeply trust each other in a world that is losing all sense of trust. Ask yourself, "How many people do I really trust? How often do I mistrust the people in my life? How many times do I have to produce credentials before people will listen to what I have to say?"

We will need such a strong relationship with Jesus that we will not be led into the antichrist's camp or his way of living. The antichrist could be on the scene today, ready to take over leadership of the world. He may well be a benevolent dictator, a great peacemaker who will serve mankind and hate Christians. His humanism is already the religion of this world. We must relate so deeply to Jesus that we will refuse the mark of the beast. Many of us believe that the Universal Product Code, which appears on every can of food you buy today, could well be that mark of the beast, and in our very near future will be essential for all who would buy or sell. I am told that this type of mark could be placed on the forehead or hand with an invisible tattoo so we could be identified easily. The tattoo ink, being radioactive, could produce twelve watts of power, easily monitored by radio. A world monetary system, based on one international credit card, which is even now being issued, will be complicated by people using the cards or having them stolen. So the next step will be needed; a body mark that cannot be lost or stolen. And where on the body would it be best located so it could not be cut off? On the forehead, as the Bible says, and, for convenience sake, on the back of the hand.

We will have to face life without that mark if we believe the Bible's warning: "If any one worships the beast and his image, and receives a mark on his forehead or upon his hand, he also will drink of the wine of the wrath of God" (Rev. 14:9, 10). What will you do when the gas tank runs dry and you don't have any cash, and you refuse to use the mark or the card or the tattoo? What will you do when the heat goes off in your home? When the food in your cupboards is all gone? How then will you live?

Many of us believe it won't be necessary to go back to the horse-and-buggy days, because by using today's technology with other believers we will have other sources of power, heat, and food. If we get together and share what we have learned and possess, we will survive. And not just survive, but possess the land until Jesus comes.

If you don't yet know Jesus as I have been trying to show Him, I want you to think about Him right now and establish a new relationship with Him. Ask Him to reveal himself to you now in all His glory. I highly recommend that you pray the following prayer:

Dear Lord, I submit my mind to the Spirit of God who dwells within me. I ask you to renew my mind, according to the promises in your Word, and grant me the mind of Jesus Christ! I ask you also, Lord, for the gift of faith, your faith, Lord Jesus, that I may understand the way you understand, and believe the way you believe!

Thank you, Jesus! In your name I pray. Amen.

5

EVERY NATURAL ACT HAS A SPIRITUAL INTENTION!

> He has by his own action given us everything that is necessary for living the truly good life, in allowing us to know the one who has called us to him, through his own glorious goodness. It is through him that God's greatest and most precious promises have become available to us men, making it possible for you to escape the inevitable disintegrations that lust produces in the world and to share God's essential nature."
>
> 2 Peter 1:3-4 (Phillips)

God made us in His image; a trinity. Just as He is Father, Son, and Spirit, so He created us to be body, soul, and spirit. There are striking implications in this truth of God.

We are not made to be just bodies. The body, left to its own devices, to its instincts and selfish desires, often follows ways of evil and perversion. But it was God's intention that what man does with his body should reflect and equip him for the fuller life of the soul and spirit. We are not made to be just souls either. The soul, when all is centered on it, can beget extreme trauma, erratic impulses and reactions. For a life lived only out of the emotions too often is a life of confusion. Nor are we made to be just spirits. To live only in terms of the spirit would take us out of life on this planet.

God made us a trinity. God built into our creation a plan for unity and beautiful harmony. The body is an important vessel for the soul and the spirit to dwell in and to which each can bring deep satisfaction, high moments of awareness of life tied into the great spiritual realms of God. Such moments are the result of each part of our lives, our bodies, our souls, and our spirits. God intends us to be in harmony. Just as the God-head is a Trinity, with the Father, Son and Spirit in total harmony and intimately related, so much so that they are one and the same, so God intends us to enter that unity of body, soul, and spirit in ways known fully only by God himself.

We have been taught, out of ignorance, that the body is a necessary evil vehicle we must learn to live with. We are taught by man's incomplete religious doctrines that we have to just grin and bear with these bodies when we can and then rejoice when at last we escape to the great beyond. The world, filled with humanistic half-truths and open lies, teaches us to just throw off our inhibitions and lustfully try to satisfy our bodies' drives, giving no thought to the future. Both concepts of living are totally in error and really blasphemies against God, the creator of our bodies. God is a God of order: all that He creates is good! If God finds joy living in a Trinity, then He made no mistake when He created us a trinity and made one important part of that trinity a body. Once we begin to comprehend that our bodies are precious creations of God (He calls them temples of the Holy Spirit), then we will realize the extreme value God places on our bodies.

Too many of us have been taught that all man has to use in this life is a hard-to-control body and a temperamental and overly emotional soul. And that's how many of us lived prior to awakening spiritually—we lived as two-dimensional people, with just bodies and souls to get us through our life, and that with great difficulty. But God created us in His image, as spirits; then He gave us souls (which include our minds) and put us in bodies. We belong together: bodies, souls and spirits. But some erroneous teachings separated us—tri-sected us—so we lost sight of our identities as God's good creation.

We are now learning that since God doesn't make mistakes, we must discover what His intentions, His plans for us as a trinity, include. What our bodies do clearly brings joy or sorrow to our souls and spirits. Our souls' reactions cause either pain or joy in our bodies. What the Holy Spirit instructs our spirits to bring to body and soul will bless and uplift them or turn them back to God when they have been allowed to debauch themselves.

Since we are the creation of a God who is Spirit, we can fully expect His Spirit to be present to make our lives remarkable according to His perfect plan. The order of our trinity should be spirit, soul, body. When that happens, a new unity of living initiates a new contentment with our bodies and souls as our spirits receive the things God intended for our joy!

But, you may say, "What about the horrible tragedies we see in our society today? People everywhere are with abandon debauching their bodies and souls with a lust that pervades all of life. We are witnessing hell on earth as people have given themselves over to orgies too ugly to even describe." This is true and I daily struggle with why people who come to us for counsel even consider living in such degradation. Fornication is now depicted on television without shame or guilt. The adulteries explicitly portrayed crowd in on us all. What men, women, boys and girls are now doing with their bodies and the tragic price they are paying in epidemics—no, plagues—is shocking! But God's intentions and plans for His creation still remain true, just waiting for believers to grasp and discover the wonder of what He has built into our *trinities*.

Let me put it more directly: God said in the Bible, in both Genesis 2:24 and Ephesians 5:31, that a man shall leave his father and mother and cleave to his wife and the two shall become one flesh. He made no mistake! Certainly in creating us with the equipment to become one flesh and then commanding that this is to be done, God didn't blow it and drop man and woman into a life sinful and dirty and unspeakable. God's intentions, when He spoke those commands to become one flesh, meant much more than just the act of sexual intercourse. God's spiritual intentions for the act of sex—what happens to the soul and spirit—are as vital to God's plan for us as the physical ecstasy. He intends the act of sex to take us to a deep commitment of love that will astound the lust-minded people of our incomplete world. The very word *cleave* implies a physical, mental, and spiritual action. "One flesh" implies a deep relationship of "one soul, one thought, one spirit," a union of man and woman in a full and wonderful life that will last into God's heaven.

But the tragedy is that too many have settled for one-or-two-dimensional lives in our mixed-up world, turning their backs on God and giving themselves over to the lusts—not the love—of their bodies and souls.

Jesus never hesitated to speak about the way man has missed God's plan and made a mess of life. He was not too embarrassed to deal in depth with the drives in man and woman, for those drives are part of the total persons Jesus was trying to bring to fullness of life under God. Jesus said, "Every man who looks at a woman lustfully has already committed adultery with her—in his heart" (Matthew 5:27 Phillips). Note well the words, "every man." He didn't speak of man in general—mankind—and He didn't include women. This is critically important. God gave man the ability to look at his wife with desire. He intentionally didn't put this in woman. God's intention for this gift to man was not to trap him and cause him to sin in adultery. Rather, this gift to appreciate beauty, to look with honor on women, was intended to give man great strength and great appreciation for his wife when life gets less than romantic. God's intention was that man look upon His creation only with true love. When God created everything, He looked upon it and saw that it was good, and built into man's mind and eye the ability to love, appreciate and honor his wife.

God gave this to man and not to woman. This doesn't imply that woman has no appreciation of beauty. In many ways, she actually has more than man. But God, in His great wisdom, created man and woman significantly different yet with their roles in life beautifully harmonized. Man was intended by God to be gregarious, able to reach out in the world, to broadly enjoy all of creation, to be a leader, able to mix with all of creation without sinning against any. On the other hand, a woman who marries and finds total contentment in being mother of life, queen of her home, her husband's helpmate, co-heir of the grace of life with her husband has eyes only for her husband and children. God graced woman with a way of life, a role that our present world laughs at and tries hard to deny and destroy. Women, deeply confused and hurt, try their best to prove they really belong in the role of man.

A very dear friend was studying Genesis 2:21-25 and questioned the Lord about His purpose in taking a rib out of man to form woman. The Lord told him that He had covered man's heart. God did not replace it, leaving it vulnerable. The woman created out of that rib is to be the covering of man's heart. Man, in his vulnerable condition, needs his loving wife at the center of his being. What an exalted position God created for woman: to cover man's heart with her great love and care so he need not lose his heart in some foolish moment of passion or stupidity, to bless him, to protect him from other women's wiles, to bring him constant love and concern.

We have failed to understand how and why God created us. In our dash to express our independence from God, we have cut ourselves off from His life. We have openly denied Him and tried every way to live without Him, cutting ourselves off from the wisdom needed for life. So we take bent ideas and demand the right to live by them. The results are daily before us.

In our ignorance of creation, we blindly enter relationships—even marriage—totally unaware of God's intentions. In our efforts to bring justice to our lives, we have brought *equality*, which we interpret to mean that there is no difference between men and women. After all, our world says, dipping again from its vast reservoir of ignorance, man and woman are identical in abilities and therefore in roles. But, noble as this appears, in our rush to make this the law of our land, we have ignored God's reason for creating us different.

As a result, well-meaning organizations and movements have arisen in our world, working against God's plan for man and woman, attempting to deny the true nature of man and woman, creating confusion in our roles. The havoc and ruin in marriages reflect mistakes due to living in ignorance of the Creator's plan.

Women and men are building their lives on ignorance and wrong conclusions, getting into error that is destroying lives and relationships. When a man fails to understand his role in relationship, he often turns away from the God-controlled life and gives himself over to lust, which, in this confused society, he calls love. He seeks satisfaction for his lusts, whereas God intended him to be the initiator of love. Fulfilling his lusts, he sins with his eyes, lusting after women, or even other men.

What God created for the good of mankind, men and women have chosen to perversely turn into something opposite.

6

YOU ARE DESTINED TO GIVE YOUR BODY TO GOD

Once there was a man who walked onto the stage of a large auditorium; many people were crowded in to see what his act would be. He wandered about the stage and kept looking all around as if searching for someone. He finally stood in the center of the stage and, looking intently at the people, asked this startling question: "Can anyone tell me who I am?" He was a victim of amnesia, and had no idea who he was.

Many of us ask that question: "Can anyone tell me who I am?" This struck a poignant part of my heart over the years, for those of us who know our Lord Jesus, the answer comes back very clearly: "You are mine! I have called you by name. You belong to me." But what about those who don't know who they are, who don't know Jesus as the Lord of their lives? To remain unaware of one's destiny in a confused world such as ours creates intolerable pressures. To face life with promise and adventure we need to know who we really are. In our hearts there should be no question of our identity, if we have found the Savior who gave us meaning for living. But too much of the world's population remains in the darkness of not knowing. They have only their best guesses as to how to live. Not knowing their true destinies and natures, their mistakes in living crowd those dear ones to the walls of despair. This ought not to be. There are clear answers from God that need to be understood. Then life for every man, woman and child can take on the characteristics God intended. Romans chapter 12 is packed with such answers.

"With eyes wide open to the mercies of God, I beg you, my

brothers, as an act of intelligent worship, to give Him your bodies, as a living sacrifice, consecrated to Him and acceptable by Him. Don't let the world around you squeeze you into its own mold, but let God remold your minds from within, so that you may prove in practice that the plan of God for you is good, meets all His demands and moves toward the goal of true maturity" (Romans 12:1-2 Phillips). I have these thoughts when I think of what it means to be destined to live a life with greater purpose than what the world today considers adequate. I have meaning in this life because I belong to God. I perform an act of intelligent worship when I give my body to God. I am a gift to God! What can this possibly mean? The world says, "You've got to be joking! What makes you think you're so great that you can say, 'Hey, look at me, I'm a gift to the world and even to God?'"

As we are giving our bodies to God in intelligent worship, think of the people who are destroying their bodies by giving them to the world! We operate a ministry in Minnesota, a discipleship camp for families and a mission to Canadian Indians in Ontario and Manitoba. Our mission is to awaken people to God's plan for their lives, which includes giving their bodies to Him. But too often we see people who have given their bodies to their own lusts and the demands of a sick world, and they are paying a high price for such living; devastation, despair, defeat, broken marriages, children running from their homes. We see people standing around scratching their heads, asking, "What happened?" We hear this day after day, and we boldly respond with what God has taught us: "Don't you understand—you've given your bodies to the wrong god! You've gotten mixed up by listening to the world's injunction to 'do your own thing.' You think you are being and expressing who you really are when you give your bodies away. But that's a lie of satan, and it is bringing destruction to millions of people."

God says the exact opposite: "As an act of intelligent worship, give me your bodies. I'll make you an instrument of worship, a joy to all heaven and to my eyes. As you give me your bodies, your souls, and your spirits, you will find the real purpose for your life. I am the one who created you and I know what will bring you total happiness." What does it say in the Bible? "You may prove in practice that the plan of God for you is good." (Romans 12:2 Phillips).

Are you consciously aware that you are to give your body not to your own selfish passions but to God? Then God can turn those passions into something beautiful! He won't remove those passions that the world glorifies so much, but He will turn them to great living according to His original plan.

I believe that speaks to young people today, to singles, to divorced people, to widows and to widowers, to people struggling with their passions in their singleness. It also speaks to us who are married. It speaks to us who would have control of our passions through disciplines rather than give those bodily passions to God so He can turn them into the meaningful drives He has intended them to be from the beginning. Do you see this? It is so important to let God receive all of who we are, everything that makes us who we are, including our bodies and their passions.

"Don't let the world around you squeeze you into its own mold." Can you picture that? Imagine people in a television melodrama caught in a car about to be crushed in a junk yard. At the last minute, someone stops the crusher, and pulls the victims out of the car just in time. That's the picture I have of the world today. In many ways it tries to squeeze us into its mold, crushing God's life out of us. We hear, "You've got to live without restraints. You've got to live as if you owned the world and have every right to do whatever you want. This is a new day free from old ways. Now you can go out and live for number one. Your body is your own; don't put restraints on it. Let it be free to express itself and do whatever feels good at the moment. God's laws are no longer applicable in our liberated society."

Think of the illusions we see on television and in the movies. I grew up with the Superman and Lone Ranger fantasies, but then stepped into a mature reality. But now, after decades of tragedies dominating the screens, we're back to childhood fantasies again because we need some illusions to relieve the pain of the sad, warped lives on display in our living rooms. Believing we can do or see anything, regardless of how ugly or violent or devious or X-rated it is, we think we should somehow come out feeling good about our lives. But the trash left our world mired in filth and sickness from it all, and fantasies are once again welcomed.

Think of what lust is producing in people's lives today. Lust was a dirty, four-letter word when I was growing up, but now it describes what is actually happening to good people everywhere. Many people are confused by the word *love* which has been so misused today. The word *love* is commonly used to describe what we know as lust. Few people understand the true meaning of the word *love* in our confused world. Most people have no idea at all of the truth; that love is fed by God, who is love. God's feeding us makes our love, and our passions too, into holy gifts to God and to each other. We need to allow God to create us again in His image with our drives directed to His purposes.

In my own denomination, the whole homosexual push, the entire feminist movement, are really nothing more than demands by depraved people for rights to have and demonstrate lust anywhere and at any time. Such demands have nothing to do with people's rights; rather, they are undisciplined caving-in to our selfish drives. Mankind is experiencing the downward pull of hell when he accepts such living as normal. But we are surrounded by a society sick unto death.

Witness: malformed babies, babies with alcoholic syndromes struggling for life, epidemic syphilis, and the horrible spread of AIDS, the ugly result of homosexual perversion.

God's word clearly describes what mankind can expect in his rush away from God. "The wages of sin is death" (Romans 6:23).

I often feel like the little boy in "The Emperor's New Clothes." Do you recall how the emperor was sold a line about having the most unusual garment ever made? The deceiving tailors who were supposedly making the garment convinced the emperor that the cloth they were using was so remarkable it was actually invisible to the common eye. No common man, after all, could be expected to be sophisticated enough to appreciate such material. The emperor, taken in by the deception, issued a royal decree that all his subjects must also believe the fantasy.

So the day came for the emperor to go out in a parade through the streets of his capital and all the people were instructed to shout and praise the king for his wisdom in wearing the most unusual garment in the world. But one little boy, a country lad, came to town and had not been clued in about the invisible clothes. When the emperor went by, this boy cried out in dismay, "Why, the king is naked as the day he was born!"

That's exactly how I feel as I see the deceptions supported sincerely by people in our world, even right in my own church. What has happened to us, loved one? We have been squeezed into the mold of a world without God, and we all are paying dearly for it. I take hope when I read of a few people speaking out against the deceptions that are creating havoc in so many lives.

The June 29, 1982 issue of *U.S. News and World Report* reported that the era of "let it all hang out" is giving way to a new, tougher approach to crime, drugs, many other social problems, that Americans in rising numbers are joining in a fight to halt the permissiveness that has spawned a host of social and moral conflicts over the past two decades. Violent crime rates, drug and alcohol abuse, laxity in school standards–these and many other ills that have spread since the early 1960's are prompting concerned citizens to forsake the benign inaction of that era and enlist in a sometimes controversial drive to strengthen authority.

God has answers to the confusion and mental anguish afflicting modern society. He stated it through Paul: "Let me remold your minds from within!" That's what God wants to do. If you have given your body to destructive forces and find yourself wounded by your foolish acts, it's time to go to God and simply say, "Here I am, Lord! I know that you're ashamed of me because of all that I have done and allowed my body to do, but, Lord, I know you can forgive me and I thank you for doing just that. But, Lord, please remold me. Remold me, Lord, for I am all out of shape!"

This request is no vain hope or illusion to keep people at least trying to live better lives. The remolding is a vital act of God through His Holy Spirit and is really a process of regeneration seldom expressed in the "instant Christianity" of today. The only way remolding can happen is for us to desire it and request it from the Father.

Then, as James said so clearly in his epistle, let the process go on. The full passage in James 1:2 and 3 expresses the attitude God wants. "When all kinds of trials and temptations crowd into your lives...don't resent them as intruders, but welcome them as friends! Realize that they come to test your faith and to produce in you the quality of endurance. But let the process go on until that endurance is fully developed, and you will find you have become men of mature character with the right sort of independence."

I can relate this process of remolding to computers. One

evening I was speaking to a group of computer programmers from IBM, Control Data and other companies. I was trying to express how God wants to remold us and I asked Jesus to give me a dramatic word for those special men present. As I started to speak, He gave me this vision:

I saw a huge computer that nearly filled a large room. Old satan was sitting on a stool right in front of the machine and he was feeding it all kinds of garbage—hate, filth, commands to do evil acts, fear, lies—and he was all excited as he keypunched all that into the machine. That computer was shaking from the junk being programmed into it. Then...in came the Holy Spirit! As he stepped into that room, satan was so anxious to get away that he knocked over the stool as he dashed off.

Then the Holy Spirit stepped up to the computer and just touched it. I thought He would probably punch the keys and go through the technical process of reprogramming such a machine. But He just touched it and I began to hear a fluttering sound that reminded me of the sound the distance-measuring equipment (DME) in a Cessna airplane makes. In one mode it indicates the ground speed of the plane. Pushing a button gets it into another mode where it starts unwinding from a high number and counts down to zero, then up to a smaller number. That smaller number indicates the estimated time of arrival. As I stood there wondering what was going on, I recalled that DME sound and a striking word Jesus had spoken to me at one moment in a Cessna 210, when, as I was watching with fascination the DME in action, I heard Jesus say clearly, "Remember this!" Now, as I was watching the Holy Spirit before that computer, that fluttering sound and Jesus' words flashed into my mind. I suddenly realized that I was hearing and watching the Holy Spirit de-program that computer. I began to grasp that the Holy Spirit was removing all the garbage satan had just fed into it.

Then I saw the Holy Spirit touch that machine again and the computer started to vibrate and shake all over. So much of the Word of God was entering it, it just shook and almost jumped with the extreme activity. People came running, asking what was wrong with the machine. Then I said, "Lord, what in the world is going to happen?"

His reply was, "This is what happens to you when my truth begins to penetrate you. Something wonderful begins and I re-program your mind from within. Now your own computer-like mind can become what it's supposed to be–a great source of my wisdom that can easily be given to others as they call forth that life-giving information."

That made great sense to me and to the computer people I shared it with in that meeting. I know that as we believers experience the Holy Spirit moving in our lives, something great begins to happen and part of that is the process of re-programming our minds—re-programming our way of looking at things and people, re-programming what we expect out of this world. Then our minds start looking at everything from God's point of view. No longer do we have to contend with "garbage in, garbage out."

Rather, "God's truth in, God's life out" to the world through us! That gives us a whole new perspective on why we are here. Channels begin to open up to God, because satan has been blown out of those channels as the Holy Spirit "makes us thoroughly clean from all that is evil" (1 John 1:9 Phillips). Then in truth we can become God's gifts to the world. As the Holy Spirit initiates and completes that process, Jesus can touch others with power through us! The eternal purpose of man and woman begins to take shape.

I no longer need to walk onto the stage of life and cry, "Who am I? What can I do? Why am I in such despair? Why did I give my body away? I don't know who I am. I have no reason for living. What's life all about, anyway?" No. Now I can walk onto that stage and shout, for all the confused world to hear, "I *know* who I am. I am a child of God! I belong to Him. Hallelujah! I'm known by name. God knows me personally! He has cleansed me from all that evil and set me on the road to real living."

The God we know remolds or re-programs us from within. The Holy Spirit sets off an implosion in our lives. The world, on the other hand, bombards us, sets off explosions from outside our lives. Both, *plosions*, to coin a word, can prompt us to quite a lot of action. But the implosion of the Holy Spirit initiates in us God's way of dealing with the world's bombardments. Instead of violent or even nonviolent reactions to the world's attacks, the Holy Spirit teaches us how to respond with wisdom from God.

As we face the world with this new power to respond instead of react, all our relationships take on a new, peaceful manner. God's "Do this and you will be saved," His "Return good for evil," His "Bless those who curse you and pray for those who despitefully use you" suddenly block out our normal worldly ways of living. We need have no more terror that the former evil in our lives might suddenly break out on people. No more foul words to try to keep from spitting out at children or wife or husband, or employer or employees, or the people down the block when we get angry. Just good things will come out, because God responds to people's anger with love.

See the striking difference? "Do not be overcome by evil, but overcome evil with good" (Romans 12:21 NAS). Phillips put it even more clearly: "Don't allow yourself to be overpowered by evil. Take the offensive—overpower evil with good!"

I'm no longer in a "crusher." I'm no longer "squeezed" by things that crowd me, because God is teaching me to be selective in what I allow to enter my life. I am learning, ever so slowly (and this is the process we have found essential in practical living), that I have the right to choose what I want to become. I can listen, and understand, and eat and drink, and do things with my body (that which is right) all because I belong to God and He teaches me how to live. He shows me wise choices. "Life by choice" means much more than choosing who will live or die. The profound implications of being free people—free to choose the right over the evil way of living—gives new power to children of the living God.

In September of 1980 I nearly died. I thought I was going to get to heaven before some of you and come back to tell the world all about it. I had open-heart surgery, then a massive staph infection. I was, in fact, dying. During that time, God spoke some exciting words to me. First he said, "Don't worry about dying. I'm going to restore you." Then He said, "You are who you are, because you are mine."

Those words keep rising up in my mind when I get discouraged or feel misunderstood or find myself feeling sorry for myself. When the world seems too much to handle, when the daily failures pile up too high, when the struggle to survive gets harder to endure, then those words come dashing forward, indicating how I am to live. I am who I am because I belong to Jesus.

In spite of all the struggles we have to face, we know that God understands and is using it all to make us over into His image. That knowledge lifts the burdens and lets life flow back into our busy and confused world. Sometimes it may seem like we don't have much to say about our destiny. But that is not the picture we will have if we know we are who we are, if we remember that we belong to God.

His hand clearly is the force behind who we are and are to become. But the God who created us to live intimately with Him knows that, to grow into full sonship, able to relate in depth to Him, we must learn responsibility. God gives us some vital actions to perform as He sets into motion His plan for our full maturity. We are required to flee from immorality. We must learn to abstain from evil. We must now cling to good! These words describe the first steps we must take in carrying responsibility.

God expects a few other acts of us. These involve our granting permission (we must have some control over our destiny to do this) for God to do dynamic works in us. We permit only God to speak to us. We let our bodies be cleansed by the Holy Spirit, so our passions can be purified. We agree that our souls should come under the control of the Holy Spirit as He awakens us spiritually to all God has planned for us. All these words—*flee*, *abstain*, *cling*, *permit*, *let* and *agree* describe the action God expects of us as we share His work of bringing our lives into harmony with His master plan. We actually glorify God in our bodies as we carry our share. God calls us to action as we choose the best for our lives and expect the best from God.

Listen now to God's profound and beautiful words preserved for us by His faithful apostle Paul:

> Let us have no imitation Christian love. Let us have a genuine break with evil and a real devotion to good. Let us have real warm affection for one another as between brothers, and a willingness to let the other man have the credit. Let us not allow slackness to spoil our work and let us keep the fires of the spirit burning, as we do our work for the Lord. Base your happiness on your hope in Christ. When trials come endure them patiently; steadfastly maintain the habit of prayer. Give freely to fellow Christians in want, never grudging a meal or a bed to those who need them. And as for those who try to make your life a misery, bless them. Don't curse, bless. Share the happiness of those who are happy, and the sorrow of those who are sad. Live in harmony with one another. Don't become snobbish but take a real interest in ordinary people. Don't become set in

your own opinions. Don't pay back a bad turn by a bad turn, to *anyone*. As far as your responsibility goes, live at peace with everyone. Never take vengeance into your own hands, my dear friends: stand back and let God punish if He will. For it is written:

Vengeance belongeth unto me: I will recompense.

And these are God's words:

If thine enemy hunger, feed him;

If he thirst, give him to drink;

For in so doing thou shalt heap coals of fire upon his head.

Don't allow yourself to be overpowered by evil. Take the offensive—overpower evil with good.

Romans 12:9-21 (Phillips)

7

THE MOST ENDANGERED SPECIES

There is nothing in more danger of extinction today than the Christian family. I have spent a lifetime counseling people from families in trouble. The past twelve years of my life have been deeply committed to a counseling center in St. Cloud, Minnesota, where we have been intimately involved in counseling over 10,000 people. We have heard problems in families that go beyond what we ever expected people to get tangled in.

When those of us who have grown up in happy families hear the problems facing American families today, we find it devastating. We keep asking, "What's happened to the American family?"

I remember too well how back in the late fifties and early sixties children began to run away from home. Many families experienced the trauma of children turning against their homes and running away to non-family situations. Haight-Ashbury in California became one center for those children. There and in many other places they were introduced to "freedom" without restraints. "Free love" (lust) was the accepted way of living; drugs and alcohol became the center of their dream world. But, deeper still, once they were hooked on drugs and sex, a new form of satan worship came to dominate their wills and, tragically, their bodies. Yes, the worship of self-will led very quickly to worship of the arch enemy of God. These young people were trying their best to get away from the core of their lives, their families. Family members had given up on each other. Fathers had abdicated their roles as the spiritual heads of their families. Mothers had given up on their children and, as they wrung their hands, they said, "Well, my child is sixteen years old. Let him do what he wants to do!"

In the early fifties there was a powerful thrust against the Body of Christ. This philosophy holds that man alone has the right to determine what he should do in any given situation, that God and His Word have absolutely nothing to do with what a man or woman should do in life. According to situation ethics, God's Word "Thou shalt not commit adultery" no longer could apply to our complex world. A CIA agent might have to seduce or let himself be seduced to get vital information for his country. "The end justifies the means "suddenly superseded the almighty and eternal Word of the living God. Life became a matter of "every man for himself" and "don't confuse me with what's right or wrong." That thrust against the truth of God, under the guise of intellectual sophistication, was even studied in churches across America. Watching this was like watching satan take an axe and hack away at the roots of that great tree, the Church. We could hear his premature shout of victory: "Timber! Watch the church fall! God doesn't really matter at all, even within the church!"

But the church of the living Christ didn't fall, even though severely threatened, because the families within the church were solid and withstood, by God's power, the axe of satan. Satan hadn't figured on believing families being strong enough to keep the church from falling.

"God-is-dead" theologians joined the attack on the church. The world and, too often, the church, espoused open rebellion and permissiveness. Mothers and fathers gave up sharing the faith with their children, saying, "They themselves will have to choose. Don't try to stuff Jesus down the throats of my children." This incredible attitude spread far and wide in many mainline churches.

When I returned from missionary service in India, after

being out of the country for nearly five years, I was often accosted by church-going people with these words: "What right do you have to get people to change their religion by stuffing Jesus down their throats?" Satan was doing a pretty thorough job of hurting the church as he attacked the Christian family. I put my life into helping families and the church join forces to launch a counterattack on satan's forces and lies.

Many of you know that God chose the 1960's to begin pouring His Holy Spirit on all flesh. It was as if God finally shouted, "Enough!" And then, instead of saying as He did before Moses on Mount Sinai, "Let me alone, that my anger may burn against them, and that I may destroy them" (Exodus 38:10), God saw fit to keep that great promise recorded in both Joel and Acts: "And it shall be in the last days...that I will pour forth of my spirit upon all mankind...and it shall be, that everyone who calls on the name of the Lord shall be saved" (Acts 2:17, 21).

How glorious it has been to see what the great outpouring of the Holy Spirit has produced! God let us experience His power in the awakening within families and individuals that has been a powerful witness to the church. A new understanding of God's order for our lives has begun to touch us all. New hope has been born in the hearts of fathers and mothers. Children have had their eyes redirected by the Holy Spirit. Many children who ran away are now home with their families or in their own Christ-centered homes! Many of the counterculture flower children and hippies have become Jesus People. We could spend many hours just recalling the wonderful work of the Holy Spirit in bringing Christian families back together. But while all this has been going on the forces of evil have not been quiet or inactive! Rather, as the power of God has awakened millions in America and the world, so the determined forces of evil have continued their attack on the home.

Permissive secular humanism has boldly joined forces with satan to unremittingly promote the death of the Christian home. "Alternate lifestyles" promote fornication and adultery. In our warped society, single parents are no longer widowed or divorced persons, but persons demanding the right to fornicate and produce children out of wedlock, who grow up without any family God can bless. Yes, even homosexuals and lesbians stand in the councils of our churches and insist on being recognized as Christians deserving of blessing from the God who hates such sin with an anger man can never endure. Secular humanism, in all its strange manifestations, is satan's attempt to destroy the Christian family and the Christian church.

There are open attacks on the Christian home under the guise of "equal rights." The mass media pick up on every aspect of this and the average citizen has a hard time figuring out the truth! Shouldn't we seek equal rights for all? An equal right to "freedom," when it ignores the Word of God and its truth, really means an equal right to sin, to steal the very meaning of life from others. As all who seek to live without restraints begin to demand anarchy, our society falls farther away from the truth. The results of such living can be measured in highway deaths from alcohol, in shattered minds of people who were free to burn their minds with drugs. The results can be measured in the skyrocketing costs of treating such *free* people. How blind we must be to be taken in by the reasoning of secular humanism so regularly endorsed by the media!

Medical practitioners have had to turn to pre-Christian philosophies to justify the murder of innocent, unborn babies, and starving to death the imperfect ones, or those old folks they consider useless and better off dead!

These are all a part of the concerted attack on the Christian family. If we fall to the attack, we will face the same wrath of God as the Israelites, who broke out of the restraints meant for their happiness and debauched themselves before the golden calf. Deviation in any form from the truth of the living God not only brings confusion and tragedy, but also warrants God's displeasure and wrath.

Having studied intimately the family and satan's attacks on it, I find myself in total agreement with the statement of a senator who is openly fighting for the American family, United States Senator Jeremiah Denton. In an interview on Ted Koppel's *Nightline* TV program, he said, "The family is one of America's most critically endangered species." In the light of this, it behooves us to seek answers from God's Word if we are to repulse the attacks on the family. For the Christian family is really a microcosm of the Christian church, and it urgently must be restored and strengthened. Jesus himself said, "Where two or three have gathered together in my name, there I am in their midst" (Matthew 18:20). To save a family of two or three believers means to save the Christian church.

8

GOD'S ORDER IN FAMILIES

Two vitally important weapons to ward off satan's attacks on the family are headship and submission. In our counseling teaching ministries we have struggled very hard with these two terms. We have studied a variety of ideas, but I write this not to express yet another viewpoint but to call into question much of what people have been taught about family relationships. Satan has used some teachings to twist our thinking, confuse our commitments and generally to weaken our resolve and discourage us. As headship has been wrongly interpreted, we've gotten bosses in our homes, instead of fathers and mothers living equally under Christ's headship. We've gotten doormats instead of mothers who bring words of love into all decisions. We've gotten people submitting to other shepherds when they had no business submitting to anyone but Jesus Christ.

By viewing tragedies in families who have blindly followed some teachings on headship and submission, I have been driven to God's Word for answers. Some may say, "Oh, here comes a Presbyterian with his 'decently and in order' doctrine." That's true! I'm still a product of what I have learned and I see much truth in God's order. Rather than debating who is the head or tail and who submits to whom, let's take a good look at God's order and all that means as we seek a deeper appreciation of "headship and submission."

Look in your Bible at Romans 12:2 (Phillips). "With eyes wide open to the mercies of God, I beg you, my brothers, as an act of intelligent worship, to give him your bodies, as a living sacrifice, consecrated to him and acceptable by him. Don't let the world around you squeeze you into its own mold, but let God remold your minds from within, so that you may prove in practice that the plan of God for you is good, meets all his demands and moves toward the goal of true maturity."

We used this verse in chapter 6; here the same words intensify the meaning of God's order, especially the meaning of submission. The very first step in getting into God's order requires submission of our lives to Jesus, so God can demonstrate His order, starting with our minds.

Submitting our minds has everything to do with our understanding of both submission and headship. Jesus is the head in whom we are to grow and find maturity. This is the crucial element people have been ignoring in this "headship and submission" controversy. We have too often forgotten that a man never really has the final word—only Jesus possesses that right!

Ephesians 6:1 reads: "Children, obey your parents in the Lord, for this is right." In verse 4, it says, "Fathers, do not provoke your children to anger." God has a way of taking care of both sides of the question. He doesn't let us get by with saying, "I've got the last word and my kids had better obey me or they'll be in serious trouble." If we read far enough in the Bible, we always find the Word speaking the whole truth. So the children have truth spoken to them, but so do the fathers just a few verses beyond. God's order is complete, never forgetting the whole family, never unjustly making it harder on one member than another. There is clear order and submission in these verses; submissive children should obey their parents, but fathers should be in such order that they do not provoke their children to anger. Rather, the fathers should follow the leading of Jesus as they teach their children with His understanding love.

I've suggested to many women that they read 1 Peter 2, which deals with wives being submissive to their husbands, but I'm always reminded by the Holy Spirit to tell the husbands to be sure and read that same passage including the seventh verse, where a strong condition is placed on getting prayers answered. The same double message of Ephesians 6 is spoken here in 1 Peter 3. Many wives say, "If my husband would just become a Christian, I could be a good, submissive wife, but I'm not going to submit to a man who is not a Christian!"

We reply, "You don't understand. You've missed the meaning of submission as it is explained in 1 Peter 3. You are to submit to Jesus through your husband. Then you can do as the Bible instructs you in this passage." We read in 1 Peter 3:1, "You wives, be submissive to your own husbands so that even if any of them are disobedient to the word (of God), they may be won without a word by the behavior of the wives, as they observe your chaste and respectful behavior."

Often men come to us for counsel and say, "My wife just doesn't understand me at all. She's driving me crazy, for she doesn't believe the way I do! She's got a hard heart."

Then we ask, "By the way, how are your prayers getting answered?" They wonder what we're talking about but finally begin to realize that, as a matter of fact, God hasn't been answering their prayers very clearly. Then we say, "We're not surprised at all, for you are not honoring your wife, and, if you're not doing that, the Bible clearly says your prayers won't be answered." Then we show them 1 Peter 3:7: "You husbands, likewise, live with your wives in an understanding way, as with a weaker vessel, since she is a woman; and grant her honor as a fellow-heir of the grace of live, so that your prayers may not be hindered."

See the interplay God's order always has? It never puts one person on top of another. It never allows the domination of one person, but too often we let our flesh affect our relationships to the point where God's order can no longer be understood.

Another truth from God's Word is found in Ephesians 4, where God has clear instructions for Christians seeking to live in His order. In Phillips' New Testament it reads: "Do not live any longer as the gentiles live. For they live blindfolded in a world of illusion, and are cut off from the life of God, through ignorance and insensitiveness" (vv. 17, 18). Can you think of anybody doing that today? Do you see anyone blindfolded, living in illusion? Aren't people everywhere stifling their consciences and daily growing more and more insensitive? "They have stifled their consciences and then surrendered themselves to sensuality, practicing any form of impurity which lust can suggest" (v. 19).

People not living under headship and not submitted to God's order in their families, their work, and their worship, are giving themselves over to sensuality and the practice of any form of impurity lust can suggest. This is why God's order clearly includes headship and submission, but in ways that protect us from the madness and tragedy of life that is "out-of-order." God calls us to a very pragmatic way of living, intended to bring great happiness to mankind. He calls us to "fling off the dirty clothes of the old way of living, which were rotted through and through with lust's illusions, and, with yourselves mentally and spiritually remade, put on the clean fresh clothes of the new life which was made by God's design for righteousness and holiness which is no illusion!" (Ephesians 4:16-24 Phillips).

In this new order, the man does not have the final word and dominate his wife and children, nor does the wife dominate the husband and children; both seek to be remade in the likeness of Jesus, in the likeness of righteousness and holiness. This is God's order for Christians.

We've already studied 1 Corinthians 2, but look at it again in light of God's order for families. Those sixteen verses lay out for the believer God's complete provision. Life takes on a whole new dimension when we let the spiritual come alive in us. With spiritual eyes we can see all that God has planned for our lives. The fourteenth verse describes our situation: "A natural man does not accept the things of the Spirit of God; for they are foolishness to him, and he cannot understand them, for they are spiritually appraised." God's Word doesn't say, "He doesn't <u>want</u> to understand what God plans for him." Rather, "He *cannot* understand." For the things of the Spirit of God are not *understood* but *discerned*. That's a different dimension of life, walking in the Spirit, awakening spiritually, becoming three-dimensional people. Becoming a trinity again. God made us spirits, gave us souls and put us in bodies. We are made in the image of God: Father, Son, Spirit. We are clearly meant to be a trinity in perfect harmony of spirit, soul and body. But too often we have lived only in two parts of our creation (bodies and souls) and most of our living has been tied up in only the body.

As families come into God's order, attitudes become remarkably different. The total man (spirit, soul, body) doesn't look at his wife just to satisfy his passions. He wants to express himself, to show his love for his wife with God's beautiful gift of sex which God meant for a great blessing. This turns life around! Human sexuality changes from a self-centered need for satisfaction into a concern to give love. Peace and order enter our home life. God's order brings a new quality to life.

God, who made us trinities, did not make any mistake. He didn't make any mistake when He made our bodies, either. Can you take everything you do physically and turn it on and off? Can you be a spiritual person part of the time and just a body when your passions arise? This is what many people are trying to do today. That's what is happening in families where headship has been misunderstood and even rejected and where submission has been abused.

Men go out and worship God and praise Him gloriously, then return to their homes and say, "OK, wife, get down here and do what I tell you to do. I've got the final word for this family." The wife goes home after worshiping almighty God and snivels around and complains about having to submit, feeling she has no rights anymore. Then women's lib may seem attractive, leading her to choose chaos over God's order. All because the husband and wife don't understand their God ordained roles. They don't understand that their bodies must submit to their spirits, and that the passions of their souls are irrevocably related to what their spirits receive from God in worship! They have so tri-sected themselves that the trinity of their lives escapes them. They compartmentalize their great moments of worship and they go back to living passionate lives minus the glory they felt in the height of worship. We are supposed to be so united in our trinities that our bodies and souls do the things we were created to do, for God's purposes and our joy.

John 1:12 speaks to this truth: "We have the right to become children of God, even to those who believe in His name." What in the world does that mean? It means we belong to God! We are His own children. We are to listen for His guidance. We are free to go to the Father and ask anything of Him. We can submit to the Father and know that He understands us completely. We then begin to inherit, as His children, His attitudes towards life. We begin to understand what Jesus was doing on the earth, and that we are to be like Jesus.

Romans 8:29 reflects this: Jesus is "the eldest of a family of many brothers" (Phillips). That's why God made us! He foreordained that we should be that way. He wants a family that submits and understands the meaning of God's headship. There really is, after all, no other head for the family of God. And, actually, there is no complete life for the children of God until they come into their own with the mind of God freeing them to life without limits.

God not only awakens us spiritually in order that we may see and receive all things He has planned for our full life, but He has made special provision for our protection by giving us the Holy Spirit. God doesn't line us up and lecture us as to our duties and then go off and leave us to work it out all by ourselves. No, He wisely pours His Holy Spirit into our lives to teach us all things and bring to remembrance all He has spoken to us.

What a practical Father! He, the most pragmatic Being in a world that prides itself on its pragmatism. That's why He gave us the Holy Spirit, to dwell in us and help us when we forget our trinities and begin living below our destinies. He promised His first disciples the Holy Spirit to teach them and remind them of His truth, and now He is fulfilling that same promise to us.

At Okontoe we have files containing about nine years of prophecies spoken to us. Many times, when I am speaking, the Spirit will say to me, "Use that prophecy I spoke to you five years ago." Then, amazingly, I can remember in detail a prophecy He wants me to use, without digging it out of our files. As clear as when they were first spoken to us, I can recall God's wonderful words, as the Holy Spirit does His remarkable work of reminding me. This, in my book, is very practical. God doesn't leave us confused, trying to remember His words for life when they are urgently needed. No, He awakens His words of life within us by the power of the Holy Spirit, teaching us their meanings.

John 15:1-17 deals with the meaning of headship and submission. We are told that we are to love one another, and that to do this we are to abide in Jesus, who *is* love. Now that's order. Our very love comes from abiding in Jesus. Love comes out of the headship of Jesus, who, in this passage, is called the vine. Love comes to us, the branches of that vine.

As a boy I used to swing on a grape vine, playing Tarzan on our farm. I swung around through the trees on the strong, muscle-like vines. Out of them grew all kinds of smaller branches. They weren't like limbs on the trees. Rather they were like the vine itself, really extensions of the larger vine. They grew right out of the vine, and, as they became bigger, they actually became the vine.

That is a perfect picture of God's order. That's submission and headship on new and understandable terms. You see, God intends not that we be limited forever to a life subject to others; rather He intends, as illustrated by the vine, that we grow as His children and one day be made over in the likeness of His Son, becoming sons and daughters of the Lord God himself. The submission and headship are for a time of growing, so God can remold us and make us into His children, full heirs of all that is His for eternity! Praise His name!

Finally, headship takes on new meaning, as does submission, when we evaluate the gifts of the Holy Spirit in 1 Corinthians 12: 7-11. God gives us gifts that connect us to Him. Think of that! Why would He do that if He didn't seek to transfer His head-knowledge to us, His children? God wants us all to have the nine gifts of the Spirit. I call them "the nine-pronged plug," as on a radio tube, meant to be plugged into God. Then we really have connections. When we get plugged into God, we are definitely in a *submitted* position, connected, submitted to what God is transferring to us through His gifts. We plug into God in an effort to hear and receive all He has planned, as our Creator, for our life. We listen to God. That's a vital part of submission: listening to what the other person is saying, whether it be a friend, a relative or God.

Have you ever thought that God needs to listen to you too? What does it say in Ephesians 5:21? "Be subject one to another in the fear of Christ." That precedes all the words about wives being subject to their husbands. That is what I see when I visualize being connected to God. There is a two-way connection between us and God. God listens to us as we listen to Him. He wants us to call upon Him. He's interested in what we're doing. His original dream for us was that we would actually be co-creators with God. That's God's plan. Paul said, "Pray without ceasing." That means constant communication with God—sharing everything with Him, submitting all our ideas and questions to Him. Asking Him about everything that crosses our minds, questioning Him in an intimate way as His children. That is the profound relationship to which He is calling us.

So submission is a two-way street. In chapter 11, I want to demonstrate how submission and even headship play vital roles in the Trinity of God. It surprised me to discover how each member of the Trinity submits to one another. It gave me a whole new concept of submission and headship when I understood that even the Godhead, the Trinity, has submission as well as headship. So this being connected to God is no small matter. It is powerful, just like having a red phone, a hot-line to God, on our desks. Then when we hear the world screaming lies at us, we can call up God and freely ask Him, "Lord, is this truth?" And often He will tell us that what is crowding us is really a lie of satan! Then, filled with His discernment, we can wake up and praise God that we escaped believing yet another lie of satan.

9

SUBMIT TO JESUS . . .
NOT TO A TEACHING OR ANOTHER'S CONTROL

Listen to Jesus, rather than just other men or ideas. So many times we are tempted to pick up on an idea, or a new teaching, and run with it and make it the center of our lives. But God won't let us do that. He says, "Come, check it out with me first." We must not submit to a certain stream of teaching, regardless of how good it appears. We must submit to Jesus, the Lord of all. Keep this in your hearts!

Then you'll feel very much at home as you go to your priest, your pastor, your husband or the person leading your prayer group. You won't feel any oppression when you say, "Pray for me. I expect God to speak to me through you." God has prepared channels for meeting Him and hearing His voice. He hasn't shut us out. He has set up an order that gives us free access to Him at all times, and that access includes our spiritual leaders. Can you see what this means to leaders, priests, pastors, husbands and others to whom people submit their ideas and turn for guidance? It puts them all in their proper positions as servants, ready to be used by God. They aren't bosses or dictators. They aren't men or women who every time have the final word for our lives. But they are servants of the living God, called to lead us to the truth—Jesus!

Lest anyone assume I am urging rebellion or a non-submitted life, let me repeat what I've already said. All of us need to submit to authority wherever we are, but within the charismatic movement certain teachings and certain extreme forms of headship and submission have been taken up by well-meaning persons and stretched out of shape. We must strike a balance between the extremes of total submission to controlling persons or totalitarian organizations, and the opposite, permissive "do your own thing" attitude. These extremes are not of God–they are hatched by satan or men and women to bring others under their control. Yes, even persons "doing their own thing" find themselves bound by their "freedom," bound by the results of their self-centered permissiveness.

God is a God of order—always—and when He reveals His perfect plan for life, it always includes clear-cut headship and submission which bring us into order and help us to live truly free from the excesses of extreme forms of teaching. Paul sums it up in Ephesians 5:21: "Be subject to one another in the fear of Christ." In other words, live under authority, submitting to each other, but always aware that God alone has the final word on how we are to live.

David clearly understood the balance we are seeking. He described its blessings in Psalm 128:

> How blessed is everyone who fears the Lord,
> Who walks in His ways.
> When you shall eat of the fruit of your hands,
> You will be happy and it will be well with you.
> Your wife shall be like a fruitful vine,
> Within your house,
> Your children like olive plants
> Around your table.
> Behold, for thus shall the man be blessed
> Who fears the Lord.

Psalm 127 is also packed with God's order for families.

> Unless the Lord builds the house,
> They labor in vain who build it;
> Unless the Lord guards the city,
> The watchman keeps awake in vain.

> It is vain for you to rise up early,
> To retire late,
> To eat the bread of painful labors;
> For He gives to His beloved even in his sleep.

We labor in vain unless the Lord builds the house, or, we could say, unless the Lord is head of the house. Unless He guards our cities—and our homes—we guard them in vain. The husband, as protector and head over his home, must be in submission to the Lord, who protects us.

And how vain it is to knock ourselves out, working late so much that our families suffer, trying to make ends meet, when God promised to take care of our every need if we seek first His kingdom—and make Him head and protector of our homes.

So many of us are workaholics, and we force that upon ourselves and our families. Our lives become *driven*. God's order is quite different: He wants to be the center of our lives. If we submit to Him, He grants the desires of our hearts. The driven feeling leaves us and God's peaceful purposes begin to flow naturally and pleasantly into our living.

Let's look at another aspect of God's order for families. Psalm 127 says: "Behold, children are a gift of the Lord; the fruit of the womb is a reward." Not a curse that a woman may escape by killing her child. What do you hear in American society today? A woman has the *right* to destroy the baby conceived within her own body. Yet the baby is a gift of God, the fruit of the womb is a reward.

But you may say, she probably conceived that baby in some loose act of sin and why should she not be able to sneak out of the responsibility by having an abortion? Certainly, many say today, it would be better for the baby not to have been born. But in God's order, could such a thing be possible? God is the Creator, not the destroyer! His order includes the results of our actions. Whether the baby is conceived by an act of sin or within marriage, a new life begins. Living out of God's order doesn't free us from the consequences of sin.

Fornication and adultery are sins against a woman's body as well as against God's order. "The fornicator sins against his own body" (1 Corinthians 6:18 NEB). Women and men have brought trouble and tragedy on themselves because they have ignored the truth.

Senator Jeremiah Denton, in *The Saturday Evening Post*, indicated that the problem isn't just abortion. The problem isn't even granting contraceptives to young girls without their parents' consent. The real problem, he said, is how we allow our children to live. Why don't we teach them to abstain from evil? Why don't we teach them to cling to good? Our families and our lawmakers are too often clearly out of God's order. This opens the door for satan to pervert our thinking as a nation, and so we Americans, known for two centuries as humane and caring people, have joined the sinful nations of the world by killing our unborn children.

God intends that we stand together as families. "Like arrows in the hand of a warrior, so are the children of one's youth" (Psalm 127:4). Arrows in the hand of a warrior...what does that mean? Arrows give strength to stand against the enemy. Does it thrill you to see families stand together, believing in each other, standing up for each other in the face of attacks? But today so many families don't stand together; in fact, they often appear to be at war with each other. Children, husbands and wives wander away from each other, and we see the wandering ones slaughtered by evil and by their own actions.

Part of our greatest sorrow comes when we counsel such people, severely hurt by their own sinful actions. You should meet the young men and women who come to us out of the drug scene, out of illicit sex lives, out of a liquor-centered and pornographic way of living. We see the dirt and filth they have been living in. They are not contented or happy, but wounded, weeping, and destroyed. For there actually is no joy or true satisfaction in lust. Such living has no promise of God's blessing, for it is clearly out of God's order.

10

SUBMISSION PROTECTS US FROM SATAN

I grew up in a family of five children, but we lost one brother when I was very little. I cherish my family and my roots more than I can express, and I want to recall again and again the wonder of our family. I know many of you come from great families and I pray you will also recall the wonder of those roots.

My darling wife and I also have had the joy of seeing our five children rise up in the fear and love of the Lord. What a joy to know that all of them and their spouses are Spirit-filled and moving in the Word of God. All are in Christian work, three of them actually working with us in our ministry. Our second son is a missionary in Indonesia with Wycliffe Bible Translators. Our fifth child, our oldest daughter and her husband were part of our counseling ministry for several years. They are now deeply involved in their church and place a high priority on raising their large Christian family.

God has brought our children together. They are like arrows. They are out in the world joining us in destroying the works of the enemy. They are standing with us for the truth of God! Together they are holding off the enemy and shutting their ears and minds to the lies that could control them. All of this happened because we as a family were led by God to stay in His order. God is the builder of the home and children are, in fact, gifts of the Lord. We can honestly say, "So are the children of one's youth. How blessed is the man whose quiver is full of them; they shall not be ashamed, when they speak with their enemies in the gate" (Psalm 127:4-5).

We have taught our children to submit to us, not by bowing to our will all the time, but by bringing their ideas to us. Yes, even bringing their girl and boy friends home for us to meet and get to know. When one of our children hesitated to bring home a friend, we often said, "If your friend can't feel at home in our family, then perhaps you ought to evaluate just what kind of a friend he is."

We tried to assure each one of our children that we wanted them to come to us at any time, even when we were sleeping, and share with us what had been happening in their lives. I remember doing the same with my parents. What a joy it was to know they cared and wanted to hear all about what we were doing! We would often ask them to share with us what kind of a time they had at school or work.

We would say, "Submit your lives to us as we submit our lives to you and taste the joy we experience together." We've had great times of good conversations as we did, and we still do this as a family. We have learned, while living in submission one to another, of the great power God gives us to protect each other and ward off satan's attacks on individuals in our family. By our acts of submission, satan's power is blocked.

Many people do not really understand God's wonderful plan to protect us from satan through submission in the family. Many people still feel that submission and living under God's authority within the family are intended just to glorify the father of the home. It actually has nothing at all to do with that.

When satan attacks, women learn to say, "I'm a woman living under God's authority…you cannot touch me." As a child of God she must be obeyed. We've seen many women protected because they told satan to go check with their spiritual head, their channel of God's protection. We know wives who phone their husbands to warn them that satan attacked them, and they say, "And don't be surprised if he comes around to you, for I sent him to you, as my spiritual head." The husband who submits to Jesus knows exactly what to do. He sends satan right on to his Head, who happens to be Jesus. Satan, of course, runs the other way. He can't go to Jesus without being exposed for the liar he really is.

One Christmas Eve, we experienced the power of such submission by our children. Our second son was engaged and growing very close to his beloved; our youngest daughter was dating a close friend. Both son and daughter were struggling with their passions. They knew that God said they must not go beyond certain limits in their love until they were married.

We had taught them well the wonder of chaste lives and the urgency of holding on to that purity in their pre-marriage relationships. We had drilled into them that to lose control of their emotions and follow their passions into sexual relations was a sin against themselves and God. And they knew well that the name for that is fornication. They understood and resisted satan's lies, as they struggled to remain faithful children of God and our faithful children as well. We trusted them fully. But as they rebuked satan and his lies, he refused to leave them. Each of them experienced this attack and found satan driving them to consider sinning.

So, in separate places and unknown to each other, they did what they were trained to do: each sent satan to their spiritual head, and each was released from that drive to sin; they escaped compromising their relationship.

That night, at two in the morning, I awoke from a sound sleep with terrible lustful thoughts racing through my head. I knew what to do: I ordered satan to get out of my thoughts in the name of Jesus, and I found myself returning to a sound and restful sleep. When the children were home for Christmas—two weeks later—my son, Don, suddenly broke into the conversation saying, "Oh, Dad, I really am sorry that I failed to phone you one night when satan got on my case. Shari and I were having a rough time resisting sexual temptation until we finally decided to send satan to you. Then we got free!"

I said, "Yes, I felt him! He came tearing into my mind and I sent him away in Jesus' name." My daughter was sitting on the other side of the table and she, being a beautiful blusher, was getting very red in the face when she said, "Daddy, I did the same thing...the very same night!" to which I replied, "Wow! I clearly got a double-barreled shot of lust that night!" The wonderful laughter that filled that room is a reminder that God has a plan for us all to have victory over the enemy wherever and whenever he strikes.

11

GOD'S ORDER FOR LIFE DEMONSTRATED IN THE TRINITY

Order in the Trinity is very clearly described in the Bible. In John 14:24, Jesus said, "The word which you hear is not Mine, but the Father's who sent Me." That's submission to the Father by Jesus. Verse 28 picks up on this same truth: "If you loved Me, you would have rejoiced, because I go to the Father; for the Father is greater than I." John 14:6 says, "I am the way, and the truth, and the life; no one comes to the Father, but through Me."

Now what does that say to you? The Father is subject to the Son, who brings people to Him, for Jesus is the *only* way to the Father. Can you see the submission between the Father and Son? Paul attempted to describe it in Ephesians 5:21: "Be subject to one another." Yet, in that relationship, the Father is clearly the greater. John 14:9 says, "Have I been so long with you, and yet you have not come to know Me, Philip? He who has seen Me has seen the Father; how do you say, 'Show us the Father?'" That says the Father and Son are one and the same. They totally submit one to another. As you look at Jesus, you see the Father; He's truly the image of the Father.

When we study the Trinity carefully, submission and headship suddenly begin to make sense! They are apparent in the Trinity, and, since we are created in God's image, God's order in the Trinity certainly belongs in the trinity of man. That order, in which God lives as Father, Son and Holy Spirit, is clearly intended for God's highest creation: man and woman, John 14:10 picks up on this: "Do you not believe that I am in the Father, and the Father in Me? The words that I say to you I do not speak on My own initiative, but the Father abiding in Me does His works."

That's also what the family is all about. That's how close, how intimate, how intertwined God wants us to be so we flow back and forth with each other. When I say, "This is my wife," I say it with joy in my heart because I love her and because all of our life together we have been subject to one another in the fear of the Lord. When you see my wife, you see me. We are not concerned about our individual rights. Rather, we find that we often think the very same thoughts…not my thoughts alone, or hers, but thoughts Jesus shares with us in our intimate relationship.

John 14:26 describes this submission to one another as the work of the Holy Spirit, whom, Jesus said, the Father would send in His name. "He will teach you all things, and bring to your remembrance all that I said to you." To teach us all things, but also to give reference to Jesus at all times. So the Holy Spirit submits to Jesus—a strange concept. This brings a new dimension to submission and headship.

John 15:26 goes on to say, "When the Helper comes, whom I will send to you from the Father…He will bear witness of Me." Now what does that say? Just above in John 14:26, we read of "the Holy Spirit, whom the Father will send in My name." Now we read of "The Helper, whom I will send to you from the Father." Jesus and the Father are so much the same, that Jesus can say, "I will send the Holy Spirit to you," or "The Father will send Him to you." John 15:27 also says that "the Spirit of truth…proceeds from the Father." But He bears witness of Jesus.

All of the above illustrates the real meaning of submission and headship. God plans for us the same wonderful relationship He himself experiences in the Trinity: our body in submission to our spirit, and our soul in submission to body and spirit. The spirit of man will be the control center, because it is the direct line to Jesus, who pours His truth down through the spirit of man into the soul and body. Then the body actually becomes a holy place (according to the Bible, a temple of the Holy Spirit) rather than a place of confusion and wanton destruction. Then the soul starts losing all its anxieties, fears and questions that too often control it.

This flow among body, soul and spirit is like the Trinity of God, and God intends that we have this same complete relationship within the Christian family too. Then the family can be the one unit with common concerns and profound relationships, making the home a place of joy and God's peace, and the family becomes stronger than any individual.

12

FORGIVENESS…THE KEY TO PROFOUND FAMILY RELATIONSHIPS

God's order for families includes learning to live together in the forgiveness of our sins. Many families we know have written off their children. We hear many parents saying, "Oh, that worthless boy had a lot of nerve to disgrace our family. After all we did for him!" Parents writing off their children. "He's of age, she's of age, they made their beds—now let them lie in them." And the children are living in hell. I see and hear this so much. No forgiveness. No understanding.

There's another side too: the most common words we hear in our counseling sessions are, "My father never said he loved me. He never once put his arm around me and expressed his love to me." Why do so many people hold back their love, maybe even proud that they are not emotional? We hear it over and over again.

"My daddy never said he loved me. He never expressed it openly. I know he must have loved me, for he beat me hard enough to make me want him to love me instead of hurting me!" We sometimes feel like saying, "Praise God he took the time to discipline you. He was at least doing that right." But how much better to see fathers, mothers, and children living together in love and in the forgiveness of their wrongs against each other!

Let me try to explain this in another way. The profound relationship God calls us to won't exist until a certain door is open for God's power and love to pass through. Being born in the same family doesn't make us love each other. My sister was one of the hardest shin-kickers I have ever known. I can remember Mary pounding my ears and kicking my shins in anger brought on by my putting earthworms down her back. My mother would stand there and say, "Children! Children, in your patience possess ye your souls!" I never really understood what Mom was saying. But we loved each other through it all.

Our love took off when Jesus took over our lives and by His Spirit opened the door of forgiveness. Our love grew over the years as my sister and I each married and we each had five wonderful children. Then our children began the process all over again as cousins; sisters and brothers kicked each other and teased the living daylights out of each other.

God wants to reconcile us. He wants to bring us together in love. He wants our relationships to grow. That cannot happen unless we forgive each other out of the depths of our hearts. Directly following the Lord's Prayer, Matthew 6:15 says, "If you do not forgive men, then your Father will not forgive your transgressions." That is surely a hard word. How do you handle that?

It's not only for your own salvation that you need to forgive and be forgiven—there is something even deeper than salvation. As we forgive and receive forgiveness, God opens the door to us too. If people do not forgive each other, the door is not open for the Holy Spirit to reconcile people. But when that door is opened by forgiveness, something great happens. It isn't just saying the words of forgiveness that brings reconciliation. It is the action of the Holy Spirit! There is a distinct difference between just saying you're sorry and believing that God himself will move to achieve reconciliation through words of forgiveness.

Some men go to their wives determined to try what we are teaching and say, "I forgive you for the horrible thing you did to me the other day." And they wonder why no forgiveness comes back from their wives. The door of forgiveness stays shut.

Others go with angry words: "Well, I guess I've got to ask for your forgiveness, so give it to me now."

The wife, still trying to handle the anger, replies, "I don't feel like giving you forgiveness."

The anger builds as the man shouts, "There you go. You're blocking anything happening between us because you won't forgive me!" The anger has control and the door is not open for love. Yes, forgiveness is more than speaking some words. It is living together in the daily forgiveness of our sins. It is living in the center of God's love and letting the Holy Spirit teach us how to live.

We've witnessed in one family three generations touched by opening the door of forgiveness, and reconciliation becoming a reality in their lives. The Holy Spirit moved on three generations because one woman believed Jesus could help her forgive her mother! Then the mother found *her* mother phoning to ask for forgiveness, all without any contact except the work of the Holy Spirit. That's power! That is the power you have to turn loose into the relationships of your own family.

If you have children turning their noses up at you saying, "You don't mean anything to me anymore. I'm going to do what I want to do from now on." That's your chance to open the door of forgiveness and let the Holy Spirit restore your family. Malachi said, "He will restore the hearts of the fathers to their children, and the hearts of the children to their fathers" (Mal. 4:6).

Below are ten lessons on forgiveness. I encourage you to study them.

1. Forgiveness is the first authority Jesus gave His disciples after His resurrection (John 20:22-23).
2. We can block our own salvation by not forgiving (Matt. 6:14-15).
3. If we fail to forgive we will be turned over to the torturers (Matt. 18:33-35).

4. The torturers are bitterness, wrath, anger, clamor, slander and malice—works of satan God allows to touch us (Eph. 4:30-31).
5. Physical illness within our families can result when we fail to live in the forgiveness of our sins (Ps. 32).
6. We can help our children, wives or husbands, brothers and sisters, as we forgive, by blocking any advantage taken by satan (2 Cor. 2:10)
7. Heaven agrees when we forgive—when we bind up satan and when we loose forgiveness (Matt. 18:18-19).
8. In the middle of prayer or worship, if you recall anything you have against another, forgive right then and there (Mark 11:25).
9. Don't give the devil any opportunity in your family's life. Clear the air before the sun goes down each day —by forgiving one another (Eph. 4:26-27).
10. Love your enemies, do good to those who hate you, bless those who curse you, pray for those who mistreat you. Whoever hits you on the cheek, offer him the other also; and whoever takes away your coat, do not withhold your shirt from him either, Give to everyone who asks of you, and whoever takes away what is yours, do not demand it back. And just as you want men to treat you, treat them in the same way (Luke 6:27-31).

I would like to illustrate some of these. Let's see what it means to be tortured when we don't forgive each other. If you're having trouble with your children sassing you or turning their backs on you, muttering, "Dumb old generation. You can't say or do anything of interest to me." you are in the hands of the torturers. If you have bitterness and hurts because of the way your children or husband and wife have treated you, you are really being tortured. If you have a feeling of anger about it and shout, "Why don't my family members understand me?" or if you say, "What they're doing is just not right! Why doesn't my husband (or wife) feel the depth of my needs?" you find anger taking over your emotions and you start swinging at your children or spouse telling them to get out of the house.

Too many parents today give such ultimatums to their children. They have no right to demand that their children get out of their homes. Children are our own flesh and blood. You can't kick your leg off if it's hurting you. You've got to take time to treat your leg if it's giving you trouble. Even so, you can let God change the relationship with your children or your wife or your husband. You can't just abdicate the role of parent or mate when trouble crowds in on you.

Is there clamor in your home—so much that you can't think? Is there hard rock music beating away, people doing their own things, eating when they want to and never being there on time when you have a beautiful meal all prepared for them? Have you wives had that happen in your home?

These are areas of torture and we are really often crushed by such experiences. Yet when forgiveness is a vital part of your life, those encounters come under control by the power of the Holy Spirit. Think of the times when your spouse came home very late and you found anger and resentment rising in your heart. Were you told, "Now don't get mad at me. I had important things to do that held me up." And instead of letting an argument get started, did you remember to open the door of forgiveness so life could go on blessed?

As that door is opened by forgiveness, the Holy Spirit rushes into the gap with healing. Then you can all share a beautiful meal and enjoy it as you are fed in more than just physical ways, for the blessings of forgiveness and the healing that follows are right then being poured into your lives.

Do you slander your children? Do you knock your wife or tell degrading stories about your "dumb old man?" I really get upset about this practice which occurs even in Christian families! God has dealt with me about this slander business. He has told me that I have no right to put anyone down—no one—especially my own flesh and blood! If you slander your own children or mate, you are really in the hands of satan's torturers who want to tear your family apart. Words of slander build up and create hatred and distrust; before people know it there is a runaway situation in the home or a divorce on the horizon. Without forgiveness in our families we welcome the forces of evil and find ourselves crowded by the torturers God wants us to escape. And the way of escape is through the door of forgiveness.

Picture yourself in the midst of an argument with your mate. My wife and I will help you picture one. One day we were caught in the middle of a quarrel before we fully understood how to shut the door on satan's torturers. (We still have quarrels but not long ones; we are learning how not to be locked out of God's love by unforgiveness for one another.) We were due at a luncheon engagement; I had had a counseling session all morning and it ran two hours late. I had gotten in that bind, knowing the counselee's deep needs, and had asked my wife to phone our friends who had invited us to lunch. She had called them and explained why we were so late and asked their forgiveness. They had assured my wife that there was no problem and that we should come when we were finished counseling.

So, two hours later I was finished, and as I was leaving the counselee's home, the hostess begged me to spend a few minutes with another friend who had come urgently requesting help. I took the few minutes, which became an hour. I finally broke away for lunch three hours late.

By the time I got in the car with my wife, she was so angry with me she could hardly talk. She had every reason to be mad at me, but I was also right, for I had obeyed God and reached out to people in need. I was also wrong in the way I began to argue with my wife. Before we knew it, as we drove to lunch, we were yelling at each other. Each of us felt unjustly attacked, and our defensiveness became wild words of bitterness.

Suddenly, in the middle of all the yelling, the Holy Spirit showed us what was happening. Satan was attempting to spoil the work Christ had done through us for the counselees. We both said, almost together, "satan, you haven't any right to do this to us! Get out in the name of Jesus!"

We reached out to each other and, as we touched each other, I said, "Darling—please forgive me—I was in the wrong."

And she said, "Oh, darling, forgive me—for I was wrong too." Immediately love flowed back into our lives and satan was clearly gone! Of course, the luncheon engagement worked out beautifully, for those dear friends had the good food in a crock-pot and understood that the ministry God had called us to share, could easily make us late. They wanted to visit with us and they made allowances for us. It was no tragedy being three hours late after all. We learned and are still learning not to give the devil any footholds in our lives.

Several years ago Jesus was teaching us in prophecy about forgiveness and how to live free of satan's attacks. He said these simple words: "Don't give the devil one moment of your time. One moment is far too much." We began to understand that we must not let satan get into our minds and start making us defend ourselves. Forgiveness disarms not only satan, but also people with whom we disagree. Think of what it means to have a daughter or son or loved friend come up and gently ask your forgiveness. What does that do to your heart? It melts me into a puddle on the ground. I want to hug and bless with all that is within me.

Harold Hill's book, *How to Live Like a King's Kid,* deeply spoke to me. I can never forget Harold's way of handling his anger while driving in heavy traffic. This has totally changed my attitude towards other drivers. He said he would start off driving along and suddenly someone would zip into his lane and cause him to brake or swerve to miss him. At such times he found himself shouting, "What's wrong with that guy? He must be crazy to do a stupid thing like that!" Then, when another ran too slowly to let Harold get through a green light (when he was already getting late for work), he would angrily shout, "Why didn't you go through fast enough for me to get through too!" He found himself in a running battle with drivers all the way to work. By the time he got to work he would look at his secretary and want to shout, "Now, what's wrong with you?" I have found myself in the same situation many times.

Harold Hill taught me to start blessing those wild drivers who were offending him by their bad and even illegal driving habits. I started praying, "God, don't let them kill themselves. Look out for them, Lord! Look out Lord, there he goes again. Please don't let him get killed or kill others!" I try to do this whenever I am driving in traffic, and it has really changed my attitude towards driving. I'm sure this has kept me from many accidents and, no doubt, protected many strangers from tragedy. Such prayers and words of blessing are acts of forgiveness. Instead of shouting, "You have no right to do that kind of crazy thing!" a word of blessing and a prayer for another's safety bring God's peace to every tense situation in our lives.

If we start living according to God's plan—blessing and not cursing, praying for others rather than being angry at them—He, the Lord of life, will bless us. As He answers our prayers for others who offend us, we begin to live—even on highways and busy city streets—in the joy of the forgiveness of our sins.

You may say, "What can I do with a person who won't listen to me?" Jesus said, "Love your enemies, bless them that curse you, do good to them that hate you, and pray for them which despitefully use you" (Matthew 3:44 KJV). That applies not only to driving on highways but even more to children and mates who no longer seem to hear our voice. God knows all our problems, and if we take our prayers to Him, asking Him to touch our loved ones with His love, as we bless and pray for them, we double the power to be reconciled, which we also use as we forgive them.

13

GOOD NEWS! OUR DESTINIES INCLUDE BEING CHILDREN OF GOD

"He came to His own, and those who were His own did not receive Him. But as many as received Him, to them He gave the right to become children of God, even to those who believe in His name" (John 1:11-12).

J.B. translated this remarkable word of God this way: "He came into the world—the world he had created—and the world failed to recognize him. He came into his own creation, and his own people would not accept him. Yet wherever men did accept him he gave them the power to become sons of God. These were the men who truly believed in him, and their birth depended not on the course of nature nor on any impulse or plan of man, but on God."

Power implies extra energy, ability to receive more than we can normally receive as natural persons. It also implies getting connected to a force outside ourselves that will somehow release power into our lives.

Let your imagination go for a moment; try to dream of what it can mean to actually become children of God, God Almighty. The Lord of all…the one who breathed life into us. God intends for us to step far beyond our humanity into the reality of being His children! This staggers my mind. The ramifications should cause us to stand in awe of the God who planned it all for us.

Children of God! That removes us from being strangers to the fullness of God and His plans for our lives. We are to be living within the courts of the Almighty, who is in charge of every moment of our lives. Think of it: endued with power to walk right up to God the Father, the Son and the Spirit, and touch the hands that bless us, doing this without fear, for we as His own children can relax in His presence—and even mess up—without fearing destruction by an old man with lightning bolts.

The power He gives us enables us to comprehend more of who the source of all power really is. We can sit at His feet and listen as He gently teaches us all things as members of His remarkable family. In the house of God we find deep appreciation for where we are and what God intends us to become. The family of God–those who are really brothers and sisters of Jesus, really sons and daughters of the Father, are intimately surrounded not only by loving friends and relatives but by that gentle teacher, the Holy Spirit.

Power. That same dynamic energizing force that raised Christ Jesus from the dead, available to us! The power that took dead cells and caused them to live again in Jesus' torn and shattered body is to be given to us so we can become children of the living God. That power caused Jesus' heart to heal and start pumping the life-giving blood which must have been transfused to Jesus by the Father himself. That same power restored torn hands and feet where the nails had done their evil work; it created new intestines and vital parts that the soldiers had so viciously ripped out of His body as it hung dying on the cross. Is it possible to grasp—even in a tiny way—the magnitude of that power? Then try to fathom God's promise to pour that same power into our lives as He makes us His children. A new excitement about what it means to be a Christian ought to touch us so deeply that our outlook on life will never be the same!

We are destined to have the same power that Jesus had as man—Son of God and Son of Man! Think of that; meditate on its meaning. Yes, God's intentions for us include being just like Jesus! He spells it out clearly in Romans 8:29-30: "God, in his foreknowledge, chose them to bear the family likeness of his Son, that he might be the eldest of a family of many brothers. He chose them long ago; when the time came he called them, he made them righteous in his sight and then lifted them to the splendor of life as his own sons" (Phillips).

We no longer need to fear being "cut off from the life of God through ignorance and insensitiveness" (Ephesians 4:18 Phillips). No more denying "God's diagnosis of our condition, cutting ourselves off from what He has to say to us" (1 John 1:10 Phillips). Open to the life God planned for us, we no longer walk in illusions but in the brilliant light of Jesus, able to live far more fulfilling lives than ever before. We can live in the joy of life...unafraid, free, not intimidated by satan or the world. We are privileged to live in the life of God himself, just as Jesus did. We are being made over into the image of Jesus. As children of God we are able to receive the things of the Spirit of God. "The fruit of the Spirit is love, joy, peace, patience, kindness, goodness, faithfulness, gentleness, self-control." That's what God intends for us.

We now share in "that sacred mystery which up till now has been hidden in every age and every generation, but which is now as clear as daylight to those who love God. They are those to whom God has planned to give a vision of the full wonder and splendor of His secret plan for the nations. And the secret is simply this: Christ in you!" (Colossians 1:26-27 Phillips)

Yes, Christ *in you* bringing with him the hope of all the glorious things to come. Can you begin to grasp the beyond imagination wonder of God as He awakens us spiritually?

God wants to give us a vision of what He knows, plans and is doing right now. We need no longer be confused by the future, for the future is in God's hands and—as His children—in ours! Understand what Paul wrote: "God has placed everything under the power of Christ and has set him up as head of everything for the Church. For the Church is his body, and in that body lives fully the one who fills the whole wide universe" (Ephesians 1:23 Phillips). As members of the Church, His body, we have His life fully within us. How do you handle that? He who *fills* the whole wide universe actually chose to stoop way down and live within us. That, to me, is the greatest miracle of all time! How can Jesus squeeze down to a size where He can actually live inside of us?

Jesus talked about what will happen to anyone who loves Him: "If anyone loves Me, he will keep My word; and My Father will love him, and We will come to him, and make Our abode with him" (John 14:23). Put that together with what Paul wrote, and you get not only Jesus, "who fills the whole wide universe," but the Father, who has no limits, both of whom want to come to us. And they plan to squeeze down to our size so they can both live within us. Add to that the Holy Spirit, whose full-time job is to fill us with himself! Hallelujah!

The day after my little four-year-old granddaughter, Christin, asked Jesus to come into her life, she walked down the stairs in her bathing suit, carrying a towel, and said to her mother, "Here goes a little girl to swim in the lake, with Jesus in her heart." Can it be said any more clearly?

In the natural sense, all we have been studying is impossible—foolish—and can't really be understood. But in the spiritual sense, all is clear. As God's remarkable plan starts quickening our bodies, souls and spirits, we find ourselves with mouths open and voices that can only shout with all the alive people of God from all times, "My God, how great thou art!" We can say with David in Psalm 16:11:

> I will bless the Lord who has counseled me;
> Indeed, my mind instructs me in the night.
> I have set the Lord continually before me;
> Because He is at my right hand,

> I will not be shaken...
> My flesh also will dwell securely.
> For Thou wilt not abandon my soul to Sheol;
> Neither wilt Thou allow Thy Holy One to see the pit,
> Thou wilt make known to me the path of life;
> In Thy presence is fullness of joy;
> In Thy right hand there are pleasures forevermore.

This truth is captured in the following excerpt from the devotional book by A.J. Russell, *God Calling*:

GOD'S FRIENDSHIP

I AM your Friend. The Companion of the dreary ways of life! I rob those ways of their greyness and horror, I transform them. Even in earthly friendships the common way, the weary way, the steep way, may seem a way to Heaven if the presence of some loved human friend transforms them.

Let the Sabbath calm enwrap your minds and hearts. Let it be a rest from the worry and fret of life, a halt by the busy highway when you see some rest and shade.

Have you ever realized the wonder of the friendship you can have with Me? Have you ever thought what it means to be able to summon at will the God of the World?

Even with a privileged visitor to an earthly king there is the palace ante-chamber, and the time must be at the pleasure of the king.

But to My subjects I have given the right to enter My Presence when you will, nay more they can summon Me to bedside, to workshop–and I am there.

Could Divine Love do more? Your nearest earthly friend cannot be with you on the instant. Your Lord your Master your Divine Friend. Yes!

When men seek to worship Me they think of the world I rule over, of creation, of mighty law and order–and then they feel the awe that precedes worship.

To you I say feel awe, feel the desire to worship Me in wondering amazement. But think too of the mighty, tender, humble condescension of My Friendship. Think of Me in the little things of everyday life.

—From *God Calling*

14

GOD WANTS US TO BE LIKE JESUS

How can we be like Jesus? Let's read Ephesians 4:17-24 and 5:5-13 from the Phillips translation.

> Do not live any longer as the gentiles live. For they live blindfolded in a world of illusion, and are cut off from the life of God through ignorance and insensitiveness. They have stifled their consciences and then surrendered themselves to sensuality, practicing any form of impurity which lust can suggest. But you have learned nothing like that from Christ, if you have really heard his voice and understood the truth that Jesus has taught you. No, what you learned was to fling off the dirty clothes of the old way of living, which were rotted through and through with lust's illusions, and, with yourselves mentally and spiritually remade, to put on the clean fresh clothes of the new life which was made by God's design for righteousness and the holiness which is no illusion.
>
> For of this much you can be quite certain: that neither the immoral nor the dirty-minded nor the covetous man (which latter is, in effect, worshiping a false god) has any inheritance in the kingdom of Christ and of God. Don't let anyone fool you on this point, however plausible his argument. It is these very things which bring down the wrath of God upon the disobedient. Live then as children of the light. The light produces in men quite the opposite of sins like these—everything that is wholesome and good and true. Let your lives be living proofs of the things which please God. Steer clear of the activities of darkness; let your lives show by contrast how dreary and futile these things are. (You know the sort of things I mean.) For light is capable of showing up everything for what it really is. It is

even possible (after all, it happened with you!) for the light to turn the thing it shines upon into light also.

Over the years I've struggled with the command "Be Christ-like." People say, "Well, you can never really succeed in this because you aren't perfect and you must get used to not being perfect. You just have to try to do things *somewhat* like Jesus did them." That gave me a lot of aches. I had read, as a teenager, Sheldon's amazing book *In His Steps,* and had tried for most of my life to answer in daily actions the question of that great book: "What would Jesus do?" I got tired of failing in that attempt until finally the Holy Spirit moved in and said, "You've got it all turned around! You don't understand. You aren't to try and somehow be like Jesus; you are to let Him *be* you!" That really rocked me. It began to turn my thinking and living around. Being Christ-like is being so open to His Spirit and His presence in your life that people will see Jesus and not just you. That's "Christ-like" in terms I can understand. And that is only possible when Jesus, through the power of His Holy Spirit, makes us righteous with His righteousness and good with His goodness. It is never only a result of our own efforts. It is by grace (Jesus' blessed and practical gift) that we are saved.

Romans 8:29 describes God's way of handling the problems of turning children of this world into children of the living God. "God, in His foreknowledge, chose (us) to bear the family likeness of His Son, that He might be the eldest of the family of many brothers" (Phillips). But while God is working on this momentous task, we are living like the world around us.

Just what is it to be *world-like* instead of *Christ-like*? Paul said it is like living in a world of illusion and, on top of that, blindfolded! What does the word *illusion* make you think about? Something sleight-of-hand? Something not really true? Something not quite what it seems to be? Or something that appears right, but is actually wrong? Can you remember visiting a hall of mirrors in an amusement park? In one mirror you appeared short and fat and in another tall and skinny. Illusions. We don't look that way in real life. What then are illusions? One definition might be: dogmatic statements that sound reasonable but really are just not true at all! I believe we all have to deal with such illusions because we live as *world-like* children rather than *Christ-like* children of God.

One such dogmatic statement is: "Wealth will inevitably bring you happiness." The world shoves this statement down our throats every day of our lives. Have you ever seen the TV program *Hart to Hart*? It is an exciting drama of action and thrills and deep emotions, but it's a total illusion. Wealthy millionaires, handsome people, loaded with everything considered to represent success, are the hero and heroine of the program. Every time they leave their home (a beautiful mansion) it is in some luxury car or sport model that would make a common man drool. One time it is a Rolls-Royce, another a Mercedes Benz or the latest station wagon. And then there is Max, the chauffeur. Everything the world dreams of possessing is there. And yet these two beautiful people are out fighting the world of crime and evil. That's the sweetest illusion I've seen on TV for a long time, and I'll admit I thoroughly enjoy being a part of their illusion. I also like the two characters in this series because they clearly demonstrate deep love for each other and real fidelity. They also show they are unselfishly committed to each other. Yet it is all an illusion created to entertain us romantics and lovers of justice.

Have you ever noticed how often the Bible seems to have the very opposite view of life from that taken by the world? What does the world say when it hears, "Turn the other cheek?" It says, "Hit him right back before he clobbers the daylights out of you. Don't give the enemy a chance"

I heard an interesting variation on this logic while I was a missionary in India. A fine Christian was traveling on a train and a fellow traveler was harassing him for being a Christian. To the surprise of the Christian, the non-Christian suddenly lashed out and smacked him on the cheek. The Christian at once retaliated with a blow that floored his opponent; as he picked himself up, he bellowed, "I thought you said you were a Christian and were supposed to turn the other cheek!" The Christian calmly replied, "Oh, no, you didn't read the Bible carefully. It reads, 'If a man strikes you on your right cheek, turn your left cheek to him also.' You hit me on the left cheek."

"It's more blessed to give than receive," says the Bible, but the world says, "It's fun to get all we can. Take care of old number one first!" God says, "No greater love has man than this: that he lay down his life for his brother." But the world says, "Don't be foolish. Don't do something stupid. You might get hurt, and if you get killed you have lost everything."

We are constantly faced with the lies, the half-truths, the assertion of rights, the beautiful illusions, all saying we can somehow be happy and successful by listening to the world. And every time we read our Bible we get a totally opposite message. So each person is faced with a dilemma until the day he says, "Lord Jesus, you are the Lord of my life and whatever you say I am going to believe, for you have the words of life!" Then a new life begins, designed by God, the Creator, not the destroyer of life. All the other advice and philosophy and bent ideas of our depraved society become known for what they are, illusions!

I'm not suggesting that we get out of this world. Satan lies about that escape all the time. This world is where God put us. But we must awaken to the truth that being *Christ-like* means living in this world but somehow not becoming a product of it, living in the world but not controlled by its illusions. Rather, we are to be controlled, gently, by the Holy Spirit, as He makes us over into the image of Jesus. When you think of living blindfolded and cut off from the life of God, the reality of what is actually happening in our world will crash in on you. If you consent to live blindfolded, you will live exactly opposite to what the Bible teaches. You will be earthbound, enslaved by lies which eventually destroy everything you do or dream of doing.

In 1976 we were trying to make the last payment on a remarkable Oldsmobile station wagon that had 160,000 miles on it. We were scraping to find the money when the Lord spoke to us on a Day of Prayer; "I know satan is trying to keep you from making this last payment and he really wants to take the car away from you, but don't worry; it is my car. I appreciate the way you've taken care of it and how you are using it and in the future I will take care of these matters for you. You don't need to buy any more cars." He further said, "You who love such things but have put them second to me will not be disappointed by what I have in mind for you."

The world says, "You've got to be kidding!" Well, the facts are as follows: God has seen fit to give Okontoe Fellowship's many families a total of fourteen cars to date, for which we asked no one but God! How do you handle such facts? Bill Gothard, in his Basic Youth Conflicts seminars, flabbergasts people by telling how God promised to provide him cars. Gothard found himself flipping through titles of seven cars that God saw fit to have people give him. We've been doing the same thing as we have allowed God to fulfill, in His own time and manner, His promises to us. God is so practical in meeting life's needs.

Yet this is exactly opposite of what the world thinks. We are going to have to learn, in these days which are the climax of history, to start living in heavenly ways. We have to drop the idea that we must always go into debt to have a car. We learned that we have credit with God. We cut all our credit cards to pieces about the same time God promised to start providing us with cars. We find it very satisfying to step into a car that has gas in it already paid for. True, we can't drive it far unless we have cash for more gas. But that stops a lot of nonsense driving and stretches dollars amazingly far.

An update on the 1972 Olds might interest you. Dozens of people in our camp and fellowship drove it—without an overhaul—until it had 203,000 miles on it. We all finally agreed to put it out to pasture because the body was nearly nonexistent. That was great fun, and I still wonder if the person who bought the car for $115 is still enjoying what's left of God's car.

When you get into Christ's way of living, everything will come into focus. I mean everything: salaries, what you are going to eat, how you are going to educate your children, how you're going to run your cars and equipment, how you are going to find homes to live in. God's mind is behind the whole universe, behind even the minute things that make up our little lives. When we receive the mind of Christ as promised in His Word, we begin to see everything from God's point of view. This is God's world, whether man and the devil think so or not! It is God's universe and we are His people, whether we are aware of it or not. And God himself created all the people of this world, whether they know it or not.

This truth came crashing in on me one day as I was burying an Indian from Canada who was not a Christian. A good friend of mine asked me to conduct the funeral of this longtime friend of his. When I found out the man wasn't a Christian, I began to wonder just how I was to conduct the funeral in an honest way. I found that his wife had once believed in Jesus and didn't deny that faith. She recognized that it would be hard for me to handle the funeral for her husband, who was not an openly confessing Christian.

I went to the funeral home, intending to read some nice

words of Scripture and preach a little Gospel message, sort of letting my conflicts of theology slide by. The funeral home was jammed with all the local dignitaries who had been friends of the deceased.

I got up to speak and nothing would come out of my mouth. Try as I would, no words would form. I just couldn't fake the funeral or give a message that would slide over the truth. Then the Lord spoke to me. He said, "Speak these words." And, believe it or not, I got a prophecy right there at the funeral. Of all times to get a prophecy...before people who never heard of such a thing. But God knew what He was doing and turned the prophecy into a short sermon, packed with His Word for that moment.

He said, "I numbered the days of this man while he was yet in his mother's womb. I breathed life into him as he was born on a canoe portage in Canada. I put him at the end of the Gunflint Trail in Canada to open up my wilderness to thousands of people, whether he was aware of it or not! Even though he didn't know me, I used him in a unique way."

I spoke these words as I wondered seriously if I was doctrinally getting out on a limb, and in fact feared that I was at the point of sawing that limb right off. I could have been speaking heresy. After all, this man had never confessed Jesus. How did I dare say words that would indicate otherwise? Yet God was indicating that this man was no stranger to Him. As I was facing that threat to my theological credibility, God continued to speak.

"For this man, whether he knew it or not, I died on the cross. I rose from the dead; I live in glory. And this man shall stand without pretense before me, your judge, and he shall be rewarded for what he did when he lived in his body, whether it was good or bad." (This last is from 2 Corinthians 5:10 Phillips.)

No one can escape God, who is the Lord of the universe.

That's why Jesus followed up with further teaching to us as He said: "Don't be angry with those nations aligned against me, just love them as I do." Our response has often been, "How can you love people who openly kill those who believe in you?" His reply was gentle; "Well, they just don't know me yet. I created them, and I'm not through with them yet. They are my creation and I have only love for what I have created."

We would certainly not choose to be blindfolded and live in a world of illusion and, because of that, be cut off from the life of God. It would be a double curse. No one in his right mind would choose it—or would he? Blindfolded…surrounded by illusions…cut off from God?

Have you ever read the story of the four blind men and the elephant? Four blind men were led into a large room where a tame elephant was tethered. The men were told they should try to tell what it was by feeling it. One brave man grabbed the trunk of the elephant and pronounced it a snake. Another put his arms around the huge leg and declared it a tree. The third walked along the side of that huge elephant, feeling the textured rough skin, and proudly said, "Why, this is a mud wall." But the last, being near the rear of the elephant, grasped its tail and with a smile called it a rope. Yes, they were all wrong, blind, living in illusions, totally unrelated to the truth. Think of this story as you evaluate where you are and what God wants you to become.

Are you a blind man, saying, "Why, this is a wall." or "This is only a tree." And then the elephant steps on you and you are destroyed. The illusions of this world destroy us because we choose to remain blindfolded. Sin is not real living. It is always a way to death. Lust always corrupts and destroys. It never brings satisfaction. Life is not just physical. It is body, soul and spirit, planned by God to be truly in the likeness of Jesus.

God has an ultimate intention for all of us as brothers and

sisters of His Son, in whose likeness God intends to remake us. He has told us in many ways and in beautiful words, "I love you with a love that you will never understand until you reign with me in glory. There's a brand-new world coming, and you are to be a part of creating it." Think of it. Sharing with Jesus the joy of creating a new world! Think of exploring the vast universe with Jesus! Think of living in a world created according to God's plans, totally beautiful, without blemish, without spot or wrinkle!

What does it mean to be Christ-like? It's waking up and finding life exactly as He said it would be. It's suddenly exclaiming, "Why didn't I see this before?"

It's at last getting connected to the God of the universe and saying for all to hear, "I belong! I'm going to go with Jesus from now on! I don't care what happens."

Jesus says to us, "I don't care whether you go bankrupt. I don't really care whether your ministries are a huge success. I care about one thing only. How you and I are getting along."

The ultimate truth, the bottom line, is that Jesus wants a vibrant, close and intimate relationship with each of us, so He can really live in us:

"Christ in you. Yes, Christ in you bringing with him the hope of all the glorious things to come." (Colossians 1:27 Phillips)

15

BUT WHY DON'T WE LOVE EACH OTHER?

In the early days of our living as a Christian community, I received a letter from a dear friend. He had watched us suffer through sharp feelings, broken relationships, and our deep questioning. He asked, "What cuts into our unity as a community of born-again Christians?" He had serious questions about the validity of even trying to live in Christian community if such sharp feelings and disunity still persisted.

After all we have studied about profound relationships, we still have to ask, "Why do we still struggle so hard to love each other?"

We suffer disunity and sharp feelings in Christian community because we greatly underestimate how much our Christian unity threatens the evil one. We are lifted up in joy by our newfound unity but often go blissfully unaware that the devil jumps hard on such times, to try to destroy us. Yet the devil has to ask God for the right to test us, and God allows the devil only a little time, and never lets him test us beyond the strength and faith He has given us. Listen to this word from A.J. Russell's *God Calling*.

"Know this...you cannot be united in your great friendship and bond to My work, and in your great love for me...and NOT excite the envy, hatred and malice of all whom you meet who are not on My side!"

You may argue, "But that's my point. I can understand strong and sharp feelings from the people of this world...but must we be hurt by people in the God Movement?" I feel more certain, day by day, that those of us in the God Movement are never at the point of total obedience to God, and, as a result, He allows the devil to try us and break us to the point where we know that, without Jesus constantly in us, we fall *out* of the God Movement.

We are still learning one big lesson daily: obedience to God's daily word to us. We must never ride along on our past successes, our spiritual highs, but moment by moment turn in total need to the Father. As long as we are in the flesh, we will always be faced with sharp feelings, and they always stem back to our failure, the physical and spiritual *impossibility* of our loving each other totally. We will perpetually fail, but Christ, by the power of His Spirit, not only forgives us, but actually loves for us and then redeems relationships that we have blown.

C.S. Lewis, in *Mere Christianity,* described this struggle all Christians face. "A Christian is *not* a man who never goes wrong, but a man who is enabled to repent and pick himself up and begin over again *after each stumble*, because the Christ-life is inside him, repairing him all the time, enabling him to repeat (in some degree) the kind of voluntary death… which Christ Himself carried out."

But back to community or church or family and the constant struggles we have to remain in love. It's hard to "kill the old man" and let the new man be born completely in us. If we expect total unity, total understanding, no hurts from those we love, we "live in a world of illusion and truth becomes a stranger to us" (1 John 1:8 Phillips). The ugly truth is that we cannot always live in a state of love and peace until the Prince of Peace comes again in power and sets up His Kingdom of peace. Still, the Christian finds peace, love and joy as he, moment by moment, surrenders to that Prince of Peace. That's the Christian life–daily surrendering, starting over again with Jesus. Jesus never promised a life here free of trouble or friction or hurt. He did, however, clearly promise us His love to overcome each of these, as He enables us to love those who are hard to love as well as to love ourselves. Jesus enters right into community when born-again Christians know this truth and when frictions come and sharp words fall from our lips. He comes when each member of a community or church or family lives so honestly, that they repent right then and there. Christ redeems each of us at that very moment of truth!

This is the heart of our community. The broken spirits we have (when pride doesn't cause us to fall) open our lives to each other, and Christ's love reaches out to heal our hurts, to rebuild relationships broken by our hard-to-bridle tongues. But one of the beautiful side benefits of community living is the closeness of our lives, allowing us to discover why we hurt and what is behind our sharp feelings; then we deal more gently with each other.

By our close living, we discover what is causing a person to be bummed out. We know when he is tired. We know why he is irritated, and because we know what is behind his sharp feelings we can make allowances. We are so close that we can easily reach out to our brother or sister, son or daughter, wife or husband in love and confront them immediately with the effects of their feelings and then, in compassion, deal with their hurts. We don't have to rely on our own ideas of why he or she is bummed out. The "lone ranger" Christians never drop their guards and so we never know them and they never experience the joy of intimate relationships as children of God!

It is wonderful to know that when we can't avoid sharp feelings, Christ in us *can* start a transformation the minute we surrender to Him. And if we think avoiding such hurts is a learned response, we are mistaken. We hurt each other less, however, in intimate community, after gradually knowing each other in depth, than is possible in our normal insulated world. This is why we believe in community. It prepares us for more compassionate and responsive ministry, and a significant part of community living is recognizing that ministry must be ongoing by the members of the community, church or family.

In community we have common goals and these allow for less conflict and more times of agreement. Our commitments are similar, too, and our experiences of worship in the presence of our Lord (especially in times of weakness) prepare us for a unity that few others ever feel or know.

The heart of it is to become so well acquainted, so free in our relationships that we really love each other, and that Christ's love enlarges ours into a real sensitivity to be felt by all others who come in contact with us.

A.J. Russell's *God Calling* for December 3, expressed how Jesus desires this closeness with us:

> Fret not your souls with puzzles that you cannot solve. The solution may never be shown you…until you have left this flesh-life! Remember what I have so often told you, "I have yet many things to say unto you, but you cannot bear them now. Only step by step and stage by stage can you proceed in your journey with Me! There does come a joy known to those who suffer with Me. But…that is not the result of suffering…but the result of the close intimacy with Me, to which suffering drove you!"

16

MY VISION OF THE CHURCH YET TO BE

On September 25, 1980, my son, Bill, left my hospital room at midnight. He had been with me through triple-bypass open-heart surgery which the doctors never believed I would survive. My heart had been about to explode from my massive coronary. I was fifty-nine and by the grace of God had survived two other attacks when I was forty-four and forty-five, back in India. Now I was facing a third attack, even though I had been miraculously healed nine years before. It looked like the end of a very complete and terribly busy life. I was about to have a vision of the Church, totally new and yet to be.

As Bill reached my daughter Suzanne's home, where he and my wife were living, he heard very clearly God speaking these words: "Get your tape recorder and go back to the hospital." Without a word, Bill got back into the car and drove across Columbus for a special appointment with God and me.

It was 1:00 a.m. when I awoke from fitful and painful sleep to find my son standing by my bed with hands upraised and beautiful tongues flowing quietly from his lips. He was, in his obedience to God, calling down the power of the Holy Spirit through whom Jesus intended to teach us new and wondrous things. He told me what God had spoken to him and said he was ready for whatever God planned to do that night. I asked him to sit on my bed and we quietly waited together for what God might do.

The first words out of my mouth were, "Isn't it wonderful to be dancing through the stars by the power of the Holy Spirit?" which Bill received by starting up the tape recorder. "You speak so softly, Lord," were the next words, indicating that Jesus was moving in to keep His appointed hour with us. "Yes, Lord, we have ears to hear and hearts to believe," came quietly out of my crackling voice. "Don't run ahead of God, for He alone is the one who energizes us. We move only by the power of God, not the best efforts of man," was gently spoken as a sort of caution I needed to say to myself and my son as we waited on the Lord.

"Isn't she a bonnie, bonnie ship? Oh, my! Strangely beautiful!"

"You see a ship?" asked Bill. "What kind of ship is it?"

"A sailing vessel."

"Where is it going?"

"Where God wills! Visions are hard to come by. They are always bigger than a man's life. Without God in our midst there can be no vision. Man can try alone but he will always fail. But when God moves, all things are possible!"

The "bonnie ship" was a gorgeous three- or four-decked sailing vessel. It was made of hardwood, like beautiful walnut and its bowsprit was a swan. As I sat on the top deck of the beautiful creation, I saw three huge masts with mammoth sails, furled because the ship was docked in a quiet cove at night on some seashore.

I recall vividly the fresh sea breezes blowing through my hair and remember how confused Bill seemed. He wasn't seeing the vision and wondered about all I was saying. As I surveyed the ship by the light of the moon, I could see the huge gunwales; the masts were so great that no half-dozen men could possibly hold hands and reach around them.

The wheel that controlled the rudder loomed huge towards the stern of that great ship, and as I examined it more closely I discovered that the spokes were so large in circumference that no human hand could possibly even begin to grasp them, let alone steer that vessel.

The ropes hanging down from the sails and yardarms

were so large that they seemed more like anchor ropes than ropes to raise and lower the vast spread of sails. In no stretch of the imagination could any sailor grasp those ropes and lift those sails! Everything about that ship was over-sized—it looked like a creation for giants.

I remember asking Jesus what kind of a vessel I was seeing. His reply was, "This is the Church! I created this ship to be indestructible and my intention was that wherever in the world people were in trouble, my ship would sail forth and save them from disaster."

I could picture this huge sailing vessel launching out across the dark waters and engaging the enemy on some distant shore or on the open sea and destroying an attack on the people of God. As I continued to ponder the meaning of what I was seeing, I asked Jesus, "How is it possible for any man to operate this ship? Everything seems made for giants, not for mere men."

He replied, "It's beyond what man himself can do. For his wholeness, man needs a touch from the finger of God. The provision of God is beyond what man can produce. It is complete and whole when man's efforts are incomplete. It can never be done (sailing the Church) out of the strength of man alone. That is why man is left strewn upon the beaches, exhausted, wondering why he was left there."

I began to put all these thoughts together with the vision of the ship I was seeing, and it suddenly made sense. The Church of Jesus Christ cannot be operated as the vessel of salvation for the people of God's world by unredeemed men. Jesus must, in His unique wisdom, touch man and actually enlarge him spiritually, so that he will be able to raise those massive sails with hands and strength far beyond his own!

I could see God touching those who believe in Him. Part of the redemption we struggle to understand includes being enlarged, strengthened, made into larger, greater men and women of God, able to operate His ship for the salvation of mankind. His words began to all tie together. We thought just a series of truths, much like Proverbs, had been spoken to us, but clearly they all fit together.

"He that is in us can regenerate that same great power that moves the spheres of God!" I said, then questioned my son, "Am I mad?" Then, "Oh yes, if I believe such can be done on the basis of what man can generate. No longer shall it be just man, but the power to steer God's Church shall be based upon what God, reaching just beyond, will *himself* create. He will make us into supermen of God! If any man be in Christ, he is a new creation altogether. It's a gift of God."

The final words Jesus spoke to us that night linger on in our memories, recalling this vision of an invincible Church whose destiny is far greater than we have ever let it be. Destined to be the Body of Christ, able to protect the world from the enemies of God. Able to reach out and save mankind. Able because men finally decided to believe in Jesus and received the touch of Jesus which enabled them to receive wholeness. The words that follow shake us daily out of our fears and lethargies as we remember vividly how Jesus spoke them to us: "Life is so much more than man will let it be!"

Let those words penetrate deeply into your spirit; discover a destiny for your life and for the life of the Church that is much more than we men and women will let it become. Recall the disappointments in churches that enthrone man as god and forget Jesus who destined the Church to be His Holy Body. Life is so much more! Think of Jesus' plan for making this a safe world in which to live; then view the mayhem and fear that rules most of this world. Life is so much more! Look at the trivial relationships that you and I settle for in our work, churches and families, and ponder; life is so much more! Let the wonder of Jesus' glorious Body overshadow you in every thought and act of every day, then come alive, let life be more, much, much more, than we have ever let it be!

The vision of the Church and its real purpose, measured against what the Church too often proves to be today, causes me to desire intently the awakening of God's people. Yes, the Church yet to be is more than the dream or hallucination of a sick man. It truly was revealed by Jesus as the *real* Church, His Body, which, when it allows Jesus to touch it again by the power of the Holy Spirit, shall become that redemptive force beyond man's greatest efforts to save the world. Then the Church of our fathers will become the Church of redeemed saints today, ready and willing to be used by Jesus for the joy and happiness of mankind.